Entering

the

Mainstream

Cultivating Mindfulness
in Everyday Life

A Manual for
Practitioners,
Teachers, and the
Simply Curious

Patricia Ullman

Sumiko

Entering the Mainstream:
Cultivating Mindfulness in Everyday Life - A Manual for
Practitioners, Teachers and the Simply Curious
Copyright © 2021 by Patricia Ullman.

Parts of this book were previously published in *Pathways Magazine* (Washington, DC, www.pathwaysmagazine.com): "Slow Food Mindfulness" (Winter 2017-18); "Family Meditation" (Summer 2018); "Finding Silence in a Noisy World" (Fall 2018); "Compassion: What the World Needs Now" (Winter 2018-19); "Mindfulness Tools for Activists" (Fall 2019).
Some sections excerpted from *Eight Steps to an Authentic Life: Ancient Wisdom for Modern Times,* by Patricia Ullman (2018).

ISBN (paperback) 978-0-578-98779-8
ISBN (ebook) 978-0-578-98780-4

Cover design by Aaxel Author Services
& Deividas Jablonskis
Interior design by Aaxel Author Services

Printed in the United States of America

To the staff and members of the Sibley Senior Association and the greater Sibley/Johns Hopkins community, for their dedication to bringing mindfulness practices into the culture of everyday life, health, and healing.

CONTENTS

INTRODUCTION

This book is intended to be the manual I wish I'd had when I moved back to the city and started my urban mindfulness journey. After years of living in smaller, quieter places, including many years at rural retreat centers, it was a shock to return to my hometown of Washington, DC five years ago.

Washington is now one of the "most overworked cities in the U.S.," according to a 2019 CNN article. Researchers based their ratings on factors like average weekly work hours, length of commute, number of vacation days taken, and how much paid family leave people are legally offered (zero). Even though I grew up here, I was struck by the crowds, the traffic, the money, and the status-conscious competitiveness. It goes without saying that it's the most relentlessly political city in the U.S., and maybe in the world. It's an exciting and exhausting place.

I returned to Washington in the summer of 2016. My marriage had finally ended, and because of the prominent positions my husband and I held in the Buddhist community in Halifax, Nova Scotia, there was a lot of fallout from our separation, which made the community toxic for me. I also felt it was time for me to come back and lend support to my 90-year-old mother.

So I carefully packed a U-Haul truck with what I would need

1

for a one-bedroom apartment in DC, and, towing my car behind, I embarked on the 1200 mile trip south. I had to pull over to cry when I crossed the border into the U.S., not only for leaving my daughter and what I considered home but also for driving into the aggression and craziness that defined the 2016 elections and political atmosphere. People I encountered along the way, including the customs officers at the border, laughed and told me I was driving in the wrong direction. But it was what I wanted to do, and, when I finally arrived, I had my truck unloaded into a storage locker and landed in a heap at my mother's house–the same house I grew up in.

It was summer in DC, and the air conditioning in the old house isn't quite a match for the swampy, sweaty Washington climate. My mother had remarried after my father died, and this second husband had become an invalid who had to live in the family room on the main floor with a hospital bed and wheelchair, and an aide who came every day. I fought my own stress and depression by walking for miles all over the old streets and parks every day, and I started writing my book about the Buddhist eight-fold path, now published as *Eight Steps to an Authentic Life: Ancient Wisdom for Modern Times*. I chose this structured topic as a means for helping my mind stay focused on something more uplifting than my own struggles and grief.

One day in August, when I was still in my nightgown, feeling hot and unmotivated to even get dressed, I half-heartedly started looking for jobs on the internet. Almost as a joke, I googled "meditation jobs dc." To my shock, two things popped up, both offering positions to experienced meditation instructors. Unheard of! The idea of being paid to teach meditation (other than a token amount at Buddhist programs) had always been a sore topic in our spiritual community, something akin to the medieval practice of selling indulgences or otherwise perverting the purity of the teachings.

So what were these ads for? There were two new meditation studios about to open, one in DC and one in nearby Bethesda, MD. Their concepts were based on similar so-called mindfulness studios in

Los Angeles and New York, which were experiencing some success with their yoga-studio-based models. They were pioneers in the new wave of the trendy mindfulness movement, entrepreneurs seeking to profit from an increasing interest in mindfulness in the U.S. And to varying degrees, they also believed in the potential of meditation to help people with things like stress and burnout. Washington seemed like a fertile place to give these ventures a try.

~

We are on the crest of an unstoppable wave of mindfulness. More and more people are learning about this ancient concept and the many benefits to be had in cultivating it.

What is mindfulness? It's the ordinary, natural ability of the human mind to pay attention to what's going on. It's a mind full of the present moment, before the thinking process starts commenting *about* the present moment. Parents give full attention to their crying children to discern what they need. It's a natural way to be. At the same time, as human beings, all of our minds wander and ruminate, taking us away from our immediate experience. So, while mindfulness is innate, our habitual thinking mind too often interferes by keeping us mindlessly absorbed in thoughts. We're only mindful when something suddenly strikes our attention, or when we make a conscious effort to be fully present and engaged.

The practice of mindfulness meditation cultivates this ability to be aware in the here and now, the living moments of our lives. The evolution of eastern traditions in our modern western culture over the last 40-50 years has finally made it possible to understand the nonreligious, human qualities of mindfulness meditation and its many neurological, physiological, and psychological benefits. With this fascinating meeting of east and west, the insight, clarity, and calm that meditators have described for eons is now being studied and validated using modern technology like MRIs. Experientially, people are realizing that mindfulness meditation not only helps with stress and anxiety, but it provides greater insight into their minds and lives. Even if we begin by thinking it will help us with stress, focus, or some other concrete goal, we will soon find it to be much more than that. Becoming reacquainted with ourselves, quiet and unoccupied, is precious.

~

The first part of this book is about mindfulness: what it is, where it comes from, who is teaching and practicing it, and how and why it affects our minds, bodies, and hearts. In the second part of the book, I describe different scenarios and techniques for teaching mindfulness meditation in corporate settings, hospitals, meditation studios, and assisted living communities, as well as to activists and to families and children. There are also chapters about compassion, pain, and the importance of silence. Throughout the book, there are practices you can use to lead groups or to do on your own, as well as instructions for working with common meditation experiences like sleepiness, agitation, boredom, and resistance.

In my journey of the last few years, I've learned a lot about "meditation without borders." By that I mean that I've come to appreciate more than I ever did before how universal the wish for happiness is, and how the act of sitting quietly on the earth is necessary for a good and full life. Beyond beliefs, beyond jargon, we are here.

I sincerely hope that this book will be a useful tool for both instructors and practitioners of meditation. I offer it with gratitude for all of my teachers.

PART ONE

Understanding Mindfulness

WHAT IS MINDFULNESS?

The essence of mindfulness is nonjudgmental attention, a mind full of the reality of the present moment without the clutter of opinions and commentary. It's a synchronization of body and mind, so that the body and mind are in precisely the same place in any given moment. We usually experience this only when something out of the ordinary catches our attention, or when we exert some particular effort to pay attention.

What scientists call our "default mode" is our usual wandering mind, with which we spend a disproportionate amount of time talking to ourselves and ruminating on past and future hopes and fears. Our minds are not aware of this present moment in which we are actually alive; our bodies are in one place, but our minds are somewhere else entirely. When we think this habitual wandering mind is the only alternative, we live our lives largely on automatic, reacting rather than responding and often feeling overwhelmed by the endless barrage of thoughts and emotions. We miss so much of our lives in this way.

Mindfulness meditation shows us an alternative, a way of freeing ourselves from our own endless cycle of conditioned thoughts, emotions, and actions. Mindfulness meditation and other mindfulness-based techniques are simple and skillful methods for cultivating this ability and developing it into our natural way of being.

So while mindfulness is an inherent quality of the mind, practices for intentionally cultivating it have not been part of the western cultural paradigm which values intellectual analysis and scientific proof over direct experience. In mindfulness meditation, we stage a gentle, intentional boycott of our usual conceptual processes (both conscious and not) of categorizing, rehashing, labeling, and judging everything. There is no criticism of our busy human mind in this practice, but simply a structured opportunity to notice the alternation between being caught in the familiar busyness and then returning repeatedly to an intentional focus, like the breath. The discipline of doing this over and over again strengthens and stabilizes our minds. There is no question that this fosters countless mental, physical, and lifestyle improvements. The Buddhists and the scientists are in agreement about this, and we're now able to actually measure many of the physiological and behavioral effects of this practice.

~

Mindfulness meditation comes from the Buddhist tradition. The historical Buddha left the comforts of his palace and studied with various ascetic yogic practitioners before concluding that he could only find the nonconceptual truth he was seeking through his own direct experience. He famously sat under a tree, vowing not to get up until he could see and understand the nature of reality beyond his limited concepts. He simply watched his mind, not buying into it, until the "veils" covering over this basic wisdom were removed and he could see things clearly. He realized that all human suffering is caused by the disjoint between our conditioned expectations and what is simply true. We can't just apply further concepts to think our way out of this predicament, but we have to sit down and unwind the web of our habitual beliefs and responses, which is a courageous, even outrageous, thing to do. It's like being able to see "out of the box," the box of our preconceptions and deeply held beliefs and biases. And while Buddhism is ultimately about helping others, we first have to see through these clouds of confusion we're constantly emitting with very little (if any) awareness of what we're doing. "First, cause no harm." "Put on your own oxygen mask first." "Clean your house." Etc. The beginning of the Buddhist path necessarily needs to be self-focused, which is not self-ish.

Understanding the different purposes of the many kinds of meditation—from simple relaxation techniques to a discipline leading to greater understanding of oneself and the nature of reality—is essential in both teaching and practicing any of them, as is the case with anything we undertake.

~

You may have heard people use the term "monkey mind," referring to our busy, chattering minds that are constantly jumping from one thing to the next. This kind of mind creates a lot of unnecessary stress, because we're constantly trying to navigate through an endless clamor of ricocheting thoughts, which sparks emotional responses in endless chain reactions. This makes it very difficult to relate fully with what's in front of us, as our attention goes in and out of focus. We miss much of our lives in this way because our eyes and ears aren't fully tuned in to what's going on around us, and this makes us feel anxious and out of control.

Mindfulness meditation helps our minds settle and become more clear. One of the Tibetan words for mindfulness meditation is *shiné* (Sanskrit: *shamatha*), which means "resting the mind," or "peaceful abiding." By taking time to stop and let your mind rest, without reacting to its jumpy profusion of habitual thoughts and feelings, you gradually settle and become more familiar with being simply present. By letting your thoughts come and go and returning to your breath again and again, you strengthen your innate ability to connect fully with what's going on around you.

In scientific terms, what's happening is that repeated input stimulates the neurons (nerve cells) in our brains, causing them to connect or reconnect and change the brain's structure and function. Depending on what we're trying to learn, that input can be mental, sensory, or physical. For example, if you're learning to play a musical instrument, the inputs are the understanding of how the instrument functions, the physical experience of how to touch or press the strings or keys, the different sounds the instrument makes depending on how it's played, and so on. Only through persistent practice–repeated input, connecting and reconnecting neurons–is the whole thing eventually coordinated and mastered.

Another traditional, less scientific way of saying this is that meditation strengthens your mind. Each time you deliberately, gently let your thoughts go and return to your breath, you're shifting your habit of letting your mind randomly drift to being able to hold it more easily and naturally on what's occurring in the present. In other words, you're less easily distracted.

A professional woman who works at home came to one of the mindfulness studios where I was teaching. She felt she needed to create a little more structure for herself and wanted to incorporate a meditation practice into her daily schedule. She has ended up being a regular meditator, mostly on her own now, and she sent me this insight: "Now I'm seeing how meditation can help with productivity. The monkey mind doesn't waste nearly as much time hopping to irrelevant topics while I try to get work done. I really appreciate the greater ease this gives my work hours."

~

The Buddhists say that true learning has to include both knowledge and experience, also sometimes referred to as wisdom and activity. A traditional image for this is the two wings of a bird, because a bird needs both of them to be able to fly. Mindfulness is a skill we can learn through understanding and practice, coupled with gentle persistence.

MEDITATION INSTRUCTION

BASIC MINDFULNESS MEDITATION INSTRUCTION

(excerpted from *Eight Steps to an Authentic Life: Ancient Wisdom for Modern Times*, by Patricia Ullman)

Short sessions of meditation done regularly are more valuable than longer sessions done only occasionally. Find a regular time in your day when you can stop for ten to twenty minutes and meditate. When you have more time, it's helpful to sit for longer periods. Finding a group to do this with is invaluable, as well as a trained meditation instructor for support.

PREPARATION

✓ Find a place in your home where you can close the door and have this time to yourself. Choose a seat that helps you to be comfortable and upright (if possible)—a cushion on the floor, or a sofa or chair. Sitting on your bed can be a good option too. If you're at work, you may be able to use a conference room or staff room if you don't have a private office. (Meditation is becoming more acceptable in many workplaces, so you might even start something!) The easier you can make it for yourself, the more likely you will be to do it regularly.

✓ Decide when you will schedule this time—first thing in the morning, midday break, before bed—whatever works best for you. But actually put it into your schedule, so that your commitment to yourself is clear. Then, if you find the time just isn't working, try another time. Every session is a fresh start.

✓ Decide how long your session will be, and stick to it. Some people like to burn a stick of incense that's the approximate length of the session they want to do, and just sit until it has finished burning. Ringing a chime or gong, actually or virtually, can also help make a clear boundary for the beginning and end of your session.

✓ Turn off your phone, completely. The environment doesn't have to be totally quiet, but the fewer distractions you have, the easier it will be to relax and be present.

POSTURE

The basic guideline is "upright and relaxed"—neither too tight nor too loose. If you have an injury, take whatever posture you need to be gentle with yourself. You can still have a wakeful attitude, even if you have to lie down. Learning to meditate is like learning a new exercise, so be sure to go easy on yourself as you get used to sitting still in this way, and stretch when you need to.

✓ Feel your seat resting firmly on your cushion or chair, so that you are stable and not perched. Comfortably cross your legs, or if you are in a chair, place your feet flat on the floor.
✓ Hold your spine in a straight and upright position, with shoulders slightly back.
✓ Relax your arms, and place your hands on your thighs, palms down.
✓ Feel the crown of your head pointing up at the sky and tuck your chin in slightly.
✓ Relax your mouth and jaw. Close your mouth and breathe through your nose, if possible.
✓ Relax your eyes. Let them remain open, gently looking down with a soft gaze. If this feels strained (you will quickly get used to it), alternate between open and closed eyes during your

meditation practice, noticing how each feels for you.

✓ Finally, feel your presence in the room, and bring your awareness in closer to your whole body, noticing and relaxing each part and then letting go. Just be present—relaxed and alert.

BREATH

Mindfulness meditation means giving your mind something to focus on, which is called the object of meditation. It is NOT (this is the only time I will use all caps) about trying to get rid of your thoughts or clear your mind. The purpose if this kind of meditation is not to find some so-called ideal, higher state of mind, but to foster a more systemic, permanent transformation—to make a friendly relationship with your own mind. Likewise, you don't need to be in any particular state of mind to meditate.

An object of meditation can be a physical object, like a candle, stone, or statue. It can be a sound, a word (like a mantra), an image (visualization), or a particular thought.

Using the breath is the most simple, natural mindfulness technique, because the breath is always happening in the here and now. It is coming from inside and outside of us, and we can feel it in our body as it happens. So it provides a somewhat more physical, present support than just a visual or mental object.

Having settled your body, turn your attention to your natural breathing. Don't try to breathe in a certain way, but be curious as each breath comes in and goes out. Rest your attention gently and precisely on your breathing. With each out breath, let go of thoughts and relax into the space around you. That's all you have to do.

THOUGHTS

Thoughts are a natural part of your mind and your meditation.

When you realize you are caught up in thoughts or feelings and have forgotten the technique, simply acknowledge that without judgment or analysis, then let it go and come back to your breath. This will happen again and again during the session, and it is this noticing—this alternation and intentional return to the object of meditation—that strengthens your ability to focus and be present. Noticing that you've been caught in a thought doesn't make you a bad meditator; it makes you a good noticer. The Buddhists say that thoughts are our friends, because they provide us with the possibility of realizing this contrast. Every time you notice you were caught in thoughts and return to the breath you are accomplishing the practice of mindfulness meditation.

MEDITATION INSTRUCTION
LABELING THOUGHTS

When you are practicing mindfulness meditation, everything that arises in your mind that takes you away from the object of meditation is regarded simply as thinking. It doesn't matter if it is a monumental or murderous thought, a vivid emotion, a song, or just habitual chatter; it's all equal in the context of meditation. You notice it at some point, acknowledge it very briefly, label it "thinking," and return to what you are doing. You don't stop to analyze or categorize the thought; you just greet it kindly and let it be, returning to your breath again and again. This is the discipline of mindfulness meditation, the gentle precision of engaging in your intended task.

Labeling thoughts is a helpful tool because it makes your meditation practice very straightforward and uncomplicated. You might be having some esoteric thought about the true nature of the mind, but in your meditation practice you just label it "thinking" and return to the breath. Anything that takes you away from your intended focus is just a thought, no matter how big or small. You are not trying to reject your thoughts or even discourage them, but when a thought arises, you acknowledge it, label it (actually saying "thinking" to yourself), and return to the breath. You take the attitude that thoughts are not a big deal.

THE MINDFULNESS MOVEMENT

Meditation is becoming more ordinary and mainstream, as the ancient practice of mindfulness meditation, in particular, co-emerges in the west as both an authentic practice and a self-help fad. Businesses are springing up all across the country that offer a variety of things under one umbrella—at mindfulness studios and in yoga classes, in schools, prisons, organizations, and businesses. The challenge that naturally comes along with that, as with many traditional things that become popularized, is how to retain clarity about its profound core even while celebrating its growing accessibility.

There is an unfortunate "fast-food mentality" in our culture, our society's habit of wanting to get a quick fix that feels good and doesn't require any work. The problem with fast food is that it ultimately leaves the body undernourished and the mind craving more. The slow food movement, on the other hand, is about remembering and honoring the benefits of real food, locally sourced, cooked at home, enjoyed sitting down. Eating in this way takes more time and attention, but it ultimately enriches one's life and health, both physically and emotionally. The analogy is a good one.

Dr. Thomas Joiner, a professor of psychology at Florida State University, described this phenomenon in a helpful way, writing that the usurpation of authentic mindfulness by the current "ersatz version" is more an issue of how it's being promoted and less to do with the practice itself. (The Washington Post: *Mindfulness would be good for you. If it weren't so selfish: How a self-help trend warped a good idea;* Aug. 25, 2017). This becomes obvious when you realize that the practice, after all, has been passed down from teacher to student for millennia, like a precious family treasure. Its methods and import are so fundamental to our integral functioning as human beings that it's actually puzzling that it isn't taught in schools and promoted as essential to our mental and physical health and development. But until recently, meditation was misunderstood as being religious or at best trippy or cult-ish.

It's likely that meditation will follow a trajectory similar to that of yoga, exercise, and running, reaching a tipping point where it will be taken for granted as part of our cultural paradigm. Yoga studios and gyms are now considered a normal feature of our American society, but not that many years ago yoga was viewed with skepticism as a hippy Hindu fad, and, before that, gyms were seen as the provenance of body-builders and wealthy narcissists. For various reasons (including, among others, the publication of scientific research confirming the many real benefits; unscientific, profit-based promotion of entrepreneurs; adoption by celebrities with resulting publicity; and the marketing of cool and sexy costumes and gear), it's now taken for granted that exercise is necessary for our basic physical health and that yoga helps keep our bodies flexible and our minds calm. Doctors routinely tell us to be sure to run, walk, or exercise. These things are as fundamental to our health as eating well and brushing our teeth.

The trade-off to these disciplines becoming so wildly popular is the uneven quality of instruction and the resulting risk of injury, frustration, or misunderstanding. The way mindfulness is being promoted can easily lead our fast-food culture to think it's another miracle drug, a magic pill for stress. As Dr. Joiner says in his article, "There's nothing wrong with pleasant activities, but those already have a name: 'pleasant activities.'"

Because of the way mindfulness is being promoted, it's natural that most people would expect to experience one of the many 'pleasant activities' being offered in the name of mindfulness, like sound bathing, visualizations involving purring kittens and wind chimes, things with exotic names like chakras, tantra, and kundalini, and instructors who talk the entire time because they're afraid to leave people with more than a few seconds of silence. There is nothing wrong with these kinds of activities (whether or not they actually qualify as meditation), but rather with the mad scramble to mush them all together under the newly-popular, scientifically-endorsed umbrella of mindfulness. (A quick internet search will tell you that mindfulness can bring a reduction in stress, less rumination on negative thoughts, more happiness and peace, improved focus, less emotional reactivity, improvement in menstrual cramping and inflammatory disorders, lower blood pressure, improved memory, increased optimism, relaxation, greater awareness, and less anxiety, fear, loneliness, and depression—and so on.) With the current promotional barrage, it's only natural that people would seek it out as something to try, another potential tool that may offer help in the ongoing struggle with this challenging human life.

~

When I teach meditation in the context of Buddhism, people have a certain idea of what they might be walking into when they come to a program or public meditation session. Images of monks sitting silently for hours on end provide a context for longer sessions and more silence, and there is a traditional language that's very helpful and acceptable in that environment.

But outside of that environment, it's important to be able to present meditation without jargon, which can be challenging even for many experienced teachers. Meeting people where they are is the only way to help them understand the value of this simple, basic practice. Those who stay with it begin to experience and understand its developmental qualities, as they become more familiar with sitting quietly and bringing their minds back to an object of focus. But that can be difficult because of the sometimes misleading way mindfulness is being hyped and commercialized.

In one mindfulness studio where I taught for a while, most people came for the usual reasons: stress, anxiety, sleep problems, and wanting to do something about the overall rat race of their lives. As usual, not that many stuck with it when they discovered it was something they had to put some effort into, unlike going for a massage or even a therapy session. But for those who did understand its value and persisted, there was great appreciation and an experience of the practice developing.

As I described previously, repeated behaviors are what's required to really learn something and internalize it. With the persistent repetition of gently, intentionally returning to the breath in mindfulness meditation, people really do begin to notice all of the effects that both the scientists and the Buddhists describe, including more awareness of their emotions, remembering where they are and what they're doing in the moment, being able to separate their thoughts and feelings from what's actually going on, not being quite so rocked by strong emotions, being able to notice and catch their habitual reactions before acting on them, and so on. But they also experience the strong side effects of the meditation, the benefits that so many are seeking: feelings of greater calm, relaxation, equanimity, and peace.

As mindfulness practice becomes more and more familiar, the technique begins to relax and become more natural. Ultimately, the point of mindfulness practice is to carry our awareness into our everyday lives, with all of our senses open and engaged. The simple technique becomes more natural and less heavy-handed, and at times even seems unnecessary.

In the same studio I just mentioned, there was a woman who

came almost every day. As the weeks went by, she became willing to try opening her eyes a little while she meditated, and we experimented with what it feels like to widen the gaze. The attitude is that life isn't a distraction but a feast, and it's not so much what comes at us as how we interact with it. Through a regular meditation practice, we can gradually gain the stability, clarity, and strength we need to be fully in the world. Rather than being constantly blown around by the winds of life's challenges, we can ride the wind with awareness, strength, and an open heart.

MEDITATION INSTRUCTION
WORKING WITH OUR SENSE PERCEPTIONS

There is an interesting balance between trying to block out the world around us and getting swept away by it. This balance is really the essence of mindfulness practice—"not too tight, not too loose." It is embodied in the meditation posture and in the light, but precise, attention to the breath or other intended object of meditation.

Our experience of the vast, mysterious world around us is limited by the structure of our particular sense perceptions: eyes, ears, nose, tongue, body, and mind. We are constantly being bombarded by infinite sights, sounds, smells, and other sensory input. Through a process that scientists call selective filtering, or selective attention, our brains organize and manage all of this for us. People whose filters don't work within the "normal" range include schizophrenics and others who experience sensory overload.

Our sense of sight is the most dominant and potentially distracting of our sense perceptions. Our attention is constantly pulled by whatever comes into our field of vision, causing us to lose awareness of ourselves in the present moment. As we receive visual input, we're instantaneously filtering and categorizing it so that the initial purity, or neutrality, of any form we see becomes almost immediately colored by our preconceptions–our particular likes and dislikes, our hopes and fears, whether or not we're hungry, or tired, or lonely–so many things.

Mindfulness exercises can help us awaken our senses and experience the world around us in a more fresh, open, and unbiased way. Here are a few:

SEEING 1

✓ Sit in a comfortable posture, close your eyes, and bring your attention into yourself: your body, your breath, your thoughts. Do this for a few minutes, deliberately reducing your awareness of the world around you.

✓ Now open your eyes suddenly with a wide, outward gaze. Enjoy the colors, shapes, and movement within your field of perception, without labeling them. Notice your tendency to start thinking about what you're doing and give things names, and return to less conceptual sight. Just do this for a little while; you can tell when it becomes too contrived. Let it go, feel your own body and breath, and enjoy your day.

✓ It's even better to do this with someone else who can guide the session, so that you are more surprised when they give the signal to open your eyes and you don't have time to think about it. Notice that first moment of openness before you start thinking about what you're seeing.

✓ If you can do this outside or in front of a window, that can provide more movement and more to look at. But ultimately it doesn't really matter.

SEEING 2

✓ In a standing position with closed eyes, connect with your body and breath for a few moments.

✓ Now, still with closed eyes, begin turning slowly, staying in touch with your own presence.

✓ Continue turning slowly until you have lost track of which direction you're facing.

✓ Stop, feel your body, and suddenly open your eyes. Relax for as long as you can in the simple visual sensation of form, color, patterns, movement. Stop when it no longer feels natural.

SEEING 3

✓ In a comfortable, seated position, begin mindfulness meditation with your eyes closed, resting your attention on your breathing. Notice how your body and mind feel as you're doing this.

✓ After a few minutes, open your eyes slightly, gazing down your nose to just a couple of feet in front of you. Continue to rest your attention on your breathing, with a slight attention on your out-breath. Do this for a while, noticing how it feels.

✓ Next, raise your gaze to about 8-10 feet in front of you. Check your posture, emphasize your out-breath, and relax. Continue to place a light attention on your out-breath, only about 25%, with the rest of your awareness on your environment. Notice how this feels, returning again and again to this relaxed but intentional technique.

✓ After a while, raise your gaze to just above the horizon and drop all technique. Just rest in simple awareness and presence for as long as it lasts. Notice your tendency to wander into thinking, and let go and relax. Stop while this is fresh and go into your day with a greater sense of spacious awareness.

LISTENING 1

✓ Settle your body and rest your attention on your breathing for a minute or so.

✓ Now shift your attention to sounds. Listen attentively, using sound as your object of meditation. When your mind wanders, just return simply to listening, extending your attention outward to sounds.

✓ Try to discern the sounds that are close and then the sounds that are farther away.

✓ Try to identify five different sounds.

✓ Listen for the tone and cadence of the sounds, rather than the conceptual content or meaning.

LISTENING 2

✓ When you're walking, listen to the sounds around you.

✓ Notice your tendency to forget and become caught in thoughts, which seem to be "in your head" as you're walking. Then just extend outward again and focus on listening to the array of sounds around you.

MEDITATION EXPERIENCE
WORKING WITH BOREDOM

Boredom is a necessary part of mindfulness training. In order to see ourselves and our world more clearly, we need to let go of our constant need for the kind of entertainment that our physical and mental activities and habits provide. Mentally, we react to moments of space, or gap, with some habitual thought, which then leads to other thoughts or actions. Whether these thoughts

24

and actions are positive or negative, we seem to prefer them to the prospect of what can feel like nothingness. Our thoughts make us feel like we exist. So it's not easy to be with our naked selves, which is why one of the terms for meditation means "making friends with yourself."

So this kind of boredom is unfamiliar. Even when we're on vacation–sitting on a beautiful beach, not doing anything in particular–our minds are still wandering and dwelling on thoughts of what might happen next, how wonderful this moment is, and of course our usual conversations with ourselves and ruminations about past experiences. In mindfulness meditation, we are intentionally sitting down and doing as close to nothing as we can get.

Because this is unfamiliar, most people come to meditation with the idea that it will be entertaining in some way: it will make them feel good, it will be interesting, and it will be something they can add to the list of good self-help things they're doing. Like our western idea of medicine as a fix that someone else can give us, it's impossible to realize that meditation takes "manual labor" and no one else can do it for you. Many people give it up and keep looking for something easier and more temporary that doesn't require so much discipline.

But true mindfulness meditation doesn't even start until you are bored with it. The realization that there is no goal other than the meditation itself, the sitting down and being with your own body, breath, and thoughts, is the beginning of your understanding and appreciation of what you're doing. It doesn't matter how glorious or hideous your thoughts, they are just regarded as thinking during the meditation session. Every time you notice your tendency to drift into habitual thoughts and then deliberately return to your breath or other object of meditation, you are loosening the hold that your habits have on you. You are learning to dwell in the cool and refreshing boredom of being simply present.

So when you feel yourself resisting the boredom, wanting to do something else, that's a good sign that something is happening in your meditation. Be kind to yourself, acknowledge your restlessness, then pause, take a deep breath, check your posture and your body for tension, and then return your attention to your gentle breathing. You're still here, just sitting and breathing. Rather than feeling like it's an insult to your habitual self, doing this is actually a welcome relief. Resting your mind in this way makes it stronger, clearer, and more resilient. It takes practice.

A BRIEF HISTORY OF
MINDFULNESS MEDITATION

Mindfulness is a basic, universal function of the human mind. Mindfulness meditation, on the other hand, is a specific meditation technique that dates back to the historical Buddha, who lived in India approximately 2500 years ago. While many traditions include some sort of meditation or contemplation–some even emphasizing silence–the Buddhist tradition codified the cultivation of mindfulness in the simple, basic practice known in Sanskrit as *shamatha,* which means taming or settling the mind. By intentionally bringing one's focus back again and again to a particular object, the habit of being present is cultivated and strengthened.

Concurrent with this, one becomes more aware of the habitual tendency to be mindlessly caught up in an array of thoughts, which foster chain reactions of emotions, actions, and more thoughts. According to the Buddhists, this web that we are continually weaving from the abundant trove of our conditioned opinions, storylines about ourselves and our world, and all sorts of hopes and fears, is what causes us to continually struggle and suffer. We are never permanently satisfied with things as they are, because they either aren't enough or we fear their loss or change. If we can wake up to the ephemeral nature of this struggle by observing it repeatedly within the formal structure of mindfulness meditation, we can liberate ourselves from the illusory cocoon that has unnecessarily confined us.

This fundamental struggle and awakening can be described in spiritual or secular terms and is the crux of where east meets west in this context. From the Buddhist perspective, the path deepens from the initial intentional mindfulness practice to a natural, effortless awareness that is free from ego-based interpretations. The Sanskrit word for this non-dual awareness is *vipashyana*, which means "clear seeing" and is often translated as "insight." Since our minds naturally possess these qualities of both mindfulness and awareness, we are cultivating, or uncovering, our true and best nature when we practice this kind of meditation. So, while it is simple and basic, it's also profound. It has the effect of cutting through our inaccurate, colored concepts about reality to the unfiltered truth, which is why it's called "clear seeing." This is none other than our inherent wisdom, the knowledge of things as they are. It requires courage and determination to walk this path.

This wisdom was closely held and preserved for thousands of years because of its importance and its potential for misinterpretation. The Buddhist view is that full realization of this truth beyond ego is not possible without the combination of dedicated practice and study– the direct personal experience of the nature of one's mind joined with an intellectual understanding of the stages and experiences along the way. Additionally, it's considered essential to have a teacher, or mentor, who has gone through this journey and can impart insights to support the practitioner who walks the path.

The unique quality of the historical Buddha is that he figured this out himself, which, for some reason, doesn't seem to happen to the rest of us. The very first thing I heard about Buddhism was that it wasn't based on blind faith, but simply involved sitting down and looking at my own mind. When I heard this, I knew instantly that it was the truth I had been searching for, a way that didn't involve having to buy into anyone else's beliefs, and I was blown away. It also seemed so simple and basic that I couldn't understand why no one had told me this before. This is why the description of this path in non-English languages doesn't refer to it as an *ism* but rather as the Buddhadharma, the teachings or way of the Buddha.

So the "goal" of this path is the path itself, the moment-by-moment observation of one's mind, being, and experience. The Buddhist teachings are voluminous in their explanations of meditation experiences as one progresses from the beginning stages to a more familiar, natural, and integrated realization; but a non-analytic experience of the present moment is the basic fuel, without which this path is just another philosophical system. So even though Buddhism has been subject to institutional calcification and corruption like any other institution, at the heart of it, in its true form, is the unbiased, open space of what may be called non-ego, non-dual wisdom, or authentic presence. This doesn't change from the beginning to the end, but is rather uncovered by the practice.

From the western scientific perspective, mindfulness is generally taught as a method for reducing anxiety and coping with pain. When we notice our thoughts and deliberately let them go, coming back to our object of meditation, there are direct and measurable effects on the brain. I talk about these more in the chapter on The Science of Mindfulness, but the point is that this new scientific research on the neurology of mindfulness corroborates the eons of experience described by practitioners. At the same time, though, the research attitude has often tended to go too far in avoiding anything that isn't measurable, or that seems too spiritual; this reductionist trend was necessary in legitimatizing the practice in our modern, scientifically minded western world. But fortunately, it's gradually becoming more acceptable to talk about the full human experience and the wish for a good and fulfilling quality of life. It will be a while before these different cultural aspects are integrated and balanced.

~

When I was interviewing for my first jobs in DC mindfulness studios,

I told the owners that I had experience teaching in public settings but that I "wouldn't take the heart out of it." What I meant was that we're all spiritual beings, capable of experiencing our world with open hearts, and I couldn't teach mindfulness as just another efficiency tool.

Spirituality is often defined as that which is beyond mere material, or relative, constructs, although it tends to be understood in the context of institutionalized, theistic religion. To be whole, we need to nurture our whole selves, and this is how I view and experience the practice of mindfulness meditation. I also acknowledge and extoll its many enormous side effects, including its beneficial effects on our sense of well-being, our ability to focus and produce, our communication skills, our mental and physical health, and so much more. But when someone sits down and simply observes their own mind, not avoiding it by filling the silence with habitual activities and thoughts, it's impossible not to notice the alternative. Whatever words are used to describe it, it's just what it is: basic space, openness, sanity, presence, being here now, non-struggle, coming home. It's something we've always known but haven't been able to verbalize or acknowledge. In this sense, we are all sacred beings, not just mechanical, secular ones.

So, I made it clear in my job interviews that I couldn't teach mindfulness as simply a tool for greater efficiency, even though it definitely can have that effect. I wasn't an entertainer whose job it is to keep people from being bored, to try to seduce them into coming back. My aim is to be kind and caring, knowing how stressed and unhappy many people are who search for these kinds of supports, and to communicate in a meaningful and relevant way. So the balance is always about being as helpful as possible: using language that makes the meditation practice accessible, connecting with what people already inherently know, respecting their intelligence, and not creeping them out with religious forms or terminology, while also not watering down the significance of the practice. I also encourage people to search around through the many resources and guided meditations that are now available online until they find something that resonates and works for them.

There is an old story about the Buddha being asked to describe in a word the essence of the Buddhist teachings. Instead of speaking, he tossed his bowl into the river and, magically, it floated upstream. In stopping and sitting down to look at your mind, you are going against the habitual flow of thoughts and feelings, deciding to step out of that river and rest on the still earth. You are taking a break from the constant and often unconscious inner dialogue, the split-second judgments and categorizing, the rumination on the past and the hopes and fears about the future. With intentionality and exertion, you can step out of that mindless flow and regain your power as a human being, the power to ride joyfully on the energy of your life - just as the Buddha did so long ago, when he left his palace and sat under a tree, determined to understand what in the world was going on.

Every time we remember to stop and breathe, to notice we're here, to step out of that river even for a moment, we are having a profound and positive effect on ourselves and on those around us. And if we can help others to understand the import of this simple practice through our example, we are helping the world.

MEDITATION INSTRUCTION
GRATITUDE PRACTICE

While gratitude is valued explicitly in many world religions, it's a basic human trait, or emotion, that can be cultivated. Not only does gratitude increase feelings of well-being and happiness, but it actually changes the brain in beneficial ways. By deliberately shifting our thoughts from a sense of unhappiness, complaint, or dullness to feelings of appreciation, we engage a different part of our brains with resulting positive effects on our immune systems, blood pressure, stress hormones, and overall mood. Disengaging from toxic thoughts and emotions to explore gratitude can also improve things like sleep, eating and exercise habits, and sociability, among others. And, amazingly, even turning your mind to the search for something to be grateful for engages a different part of the brain and provides that same benefit. You can feel the shift when you do this, like stepping out of a dark room to look at the bright, open sky.

Presenting gratitude practices can be tricky because of the religious or "love and lighty" associations, and also because there are cultural differences among people and nationalities. But when done properly, with a light touch and scientific/experiential explanation, I have found that it really makes sense to people.

Here are a few ways, among countless others, of practicing gratitude:

- ✓ At a certain time each day (generally morning or evening), think of three things you're grateful for and write them down. You can do this on your own, or exchange daily text messages with a friend.
- ✓ At the beginning or end of a meditation session, contemplate your good fortune in having the circumstances to meditate, like your health, your relatively peaceful and safe environment, time to pursue something beyond mere survival, etc.
- ✓ Appreciate the sights, sounds, smells, and textures of nature when you walk.
- ✓ Stop before eating and appreciate the many factors that were necessary to bring your food to your plate.
- ✓ Notice when you are mentally complaining and see if you can turn your mind toward gratitude instead.
- ✓ Appreciate the strengths of others rather than focusing on their weaknesses.
- ✓ Notice other people's acts of kindness and thank them if

possible, or at least consciously appreciate them.

✓ What are you grateful for about your physical body? Your mind? Your circumstances? (This is an especially good contemplation for a guided group. It can also be done in pairs or triads, with the group leader timing. Each person in the pair can speak for a couple of minutes or so, then pause, give the next instruction and time to contemplate it, then each person speaks about it, etc. This can also be coupled with mindful listening practice.) At the end, radiate out your feeling of gratitude to the others in the room, and to the whole world. Then let it dissolve into your heart, remaining there, and return to the simplicity of your own breath.

MINDFULNESS INSTRUCTORS

W hat (in the world) are the qualifications for calling oneself a meditation instructor? What is the difference between teaching meditation and simply guiding a visualization or relaxation technique? There are probably as many answers to these questions as there are people teaching and guiding meditators around the world, but I think it comes down to the same thing as the basic meditation instruction: not too tight, not too loose. It's important for this basic human practice to be as accessible as possible without diminishing its purpose and effectiveness. My own journey has led me to this view.

Since first becoming a Buddhist, I had always taken it for granted that careful training and permission were required for certification as a meditation instructor. But in the new world of accessible mindfulness, I was somewhat of an anomaly, and the meditation studios that hired me were fascinated by the depth of my meditation background in comparison with most of the other instructors. As one of those old Buddhists who connected with a teacher in the 1970s, I had followed the strict and traditional path dictated by that tradition.

Back then, there were few books and fewer teachers. I was fortunate at that time to meet a real Tibetan Buddhist teacher, the first one to come to the west following the escalation of the Tibetan cultural genocide and resulting diaspora. Chögyam Trungpa landed in quite a different culture than he was used to, and he was struck by our tendency to want a bandaid approach to spirituality, something painless and superficial, dressed up in exotica and flashy credentials. One of the first books he published in the west was called *Cutting Through Spiritual Materialism*, a treatise about the gross and subtle ways in which we deceive ourselves, and a description of how to unwind this web and awaken to a less ego-centered existence. He always stressed that walking on the path of personal awakening is manual labor that no one else can accomplish for you. I was a personal student of Trungpa Rinpoche until his death in 1987 and then continued my studies with other teachers.

Trungpa Rinpoche's requirements for becoming a meditation instructor were strict and demanding. We had to complete a dathün (a month-long meditation retreat, which also had prerequisites), a three-month seminary (which had stringent practice and study entry requirements and exams), and the preliminary vajrayana practices known as *ngöndro* (100,000 physical prostrations with a liturgy and visualization, 100,000 purification mantras, 100,000 mandala offerings, and 1 million devotional mantras), which were preparation for full vajrayana empowerment, or *abhisheka*. There was then a rigorous meditation instructor training program, complete with memorization, simulated interviews with feedback, oral and written tests, a trial period, and ongoing levels of authorization requiring continuing study and examination. At a gathering in Boston in 1978, Trungpa Rinpoche called us all in for a special meeting and told us that we were his lineage holders, placing his ritual *dorje* on our heads as we filed by and knelt for this profound empowerment.

Now there are countless opportunities to learn how to be a meditation instructor (including just saying that you are). There are long and short programs, in-person and on-line. Many of these wisely require that participants complete a certain amount of meditation practice as part of the training. But because it seems so simple, there are many others who don't understand the subtleties that can only be gained through personal experience. I've met countless instructors in many different contexts, and I would say that most of them are wonderful people with the best of intentions. But the depth of their own experience is all over the place, and this becomes important when guiding people who are sitting quietly with themselves, often for the first time. Many experiences and questions naturally arise.

My niece, a fourth-year medical student, recently had the opportunity to attend a special class on meditation as part of her school's alternative medicine section. It was a short one-off session, and when she commented after the guided meditation that she kept falling asleep and couldn't concentrate on her breath, the instructor told her that she was doing it wrong and needed to try harder. My niece left feeling that she wasn't the kind of person who could meditate or who would be helped by meditation. This is a classic example of how a poorly trained instructor can harm rather than help someone by holding herself out as an expert. Who knows how many people she and others like her have turned away from meditation?

So the challenge is to be nondogmatic but genuine, and to present meditation in a way that can resonate with people of diverse backgrounds and circumstances. I have definitely floundered at times, wondering how to help people who show up looking for quick relief from their anxiety. I've learned to add a bit more guidance through the meditation sessions, but if people have been coming regularly I like to challenge them with longer periods of silence, which most of them seem to understand, appreciate, and feel empowered by. At times I feel I talk too much, at times too little. There is no way to predict who will be at any particular session, so my goal is to make it meaningful for whoever is there—not always achievable because of the wide range of expectations. I've been touched by the many people who've come through the doors in search of some peace–only a handful of whom stick it out, because meditation is so boring! But the ones who keep coming really start to see how it benefits them.

~

Here are some of the basic aspects of teaching meditation in a secular setting:

✓ Guiding meditation requires the instructor to be aware of and sensitive to the environment. The room should be set up before the session starts, with attention to arrangement, lighting, and other factors that contribute to comfort and ambience (like noise, clutter, privacy, etc.). Each situation may offer its own strengths and weakness, but it's rare that a space would be totally unworkable. If you're in a situation that has meditation cushions, make sure there are also chairs for people who can't or don't want to sit on the floor.

✓ Sensitivity to the participants is paramount, and helping them to feel at ease is essential to their being able to relax and focus on the meditation. Many people are walking into an unknown situation, which takes quite a lot of courage no matter how curious they are. So an instructor who is friendly, reassuring, and attentive to the needs of the participants is much more effective and helpful than one who is nervous and self-conscious. This is about them, not about you.

✓ Explaining the basis for the session—what it is, how it helps people, why it's important, etc.—respects and engages people intellectually and helps motivate them. Most people don't understand that there are many kinds of meditation, what distinguishes mindfulness from the others, why there is so much scientific interest and research about it, and so on. I often mention a current news article about something related to mindfulness (of which there are many, and often!). It's important to give a little context to what they're about to do, without talking too much.

✓ Begin with body and posture, making sure people are comfortable and helping anyone with a particular physical issue to adjust as needed. Make sure they know they can move if they need to (many people think that meditators need to be perfectly still) and describe the basic posture. Be sure you're modeling the posture through the session. Then, guide the session in whatever way you've decided, keeping an eye on the participants from time to time to see how they're doing. It's best if you aren't fixated on doing a canned 'routine,' but that you're able to use your experience to provide what's needed and be present with the energy of the group. If the person or group attends regularly, you can gradually extend the duration of silence between your simple instructions.

✓ After you close, be sure to thank everyone and let them know they can ask questions any time. Many people aren't comfortable (yet) asking a question in front of everyone, so you can say that you'll be available for a few minutes afterward. It's also good to end a session a few minutes before the ending time, so there is time for questions and comments.

MEDITATION INSTRUCTION
GUIDED MEDITATION

This is just a guideline that you can use and embellish in any way that feels appropriate. Gongs to begin and end are nice if appropriate, but not necessary.

After welcoming everyone and ensuring that they're seated comfortably:

Take a nice, deep breath, and gather your attention in to yourself: feel your body, seated on your chair/cushion, right here in this room... Bring your attention in to your body and notice how you're feeling. You may feel awash in thoughts and sensations about where you just came from, perhaps rushing to get here, pulling yourself away from what you were doing... Take a nice, slow breath in through your nose, down into your whole body. Let go of your thoughts about where you just came from, or what you have to do next, and give yourself this time to check in and really be here, where you are, right now...

Close your eyes or leave them open a little with a soft, downward gaze, whichever you like...

Feel your body breathing... then make your breathing slightly slower and deeper, but not at all strained...

Notice your posture: feet resting on the floor (or, if on a cushion, legs comfortably crossed); hands resting on your legs or in your lap; upright, relaxed spine, rising up toward the sky above you...

Now take a moment and feel the stillness of stopping to rest on the earth, after all of your usual mental and physical activity....

Now we'll do a mindful scan of our bodies, noticing the different parts of ourselves, what they're feeling, and whether we're subconsciously holding tension anywhere:

Bring your attention to your face. First, notice how your eyes are feeling... Soften and relax the muscles in and around your eyes... your eyebrows, and your forehead....

[continue with body scan over the whole body, down to the feet and toes]

Feel the presence of your whole body, right here. As you inhale gently through your nose, bring your attention down from your head into your torso, feeling your body move gently with each in-breath and each out-breath. Take a break from your thoughts, and just feel your body breathing....

Rest your mind as you follow each breath in, each breath

out....

When you notice you've been caught up in thoughts, simply acknowledge that without any need to analyze, and come back to the simple and peaceful awareness of your breathing....

Let your thoughts come and go, keeping your breath in the forefront of your attention....

[Include as much guidance and as much silence as appropriate.]

As we begin to close, you can open your eyes a little, when you're ready.... Bring your awareness back to yourself.... notice your posture, and scan over your body to check for any tensions, and relax.... Notice your breath again.... Feel the air on your skin.... listen to the sounds around you....

And then start to move and stretch a little, and begin to widen your gaze....

Thank you.

MINDFULNESS PRACTITIONERS

A colleague of mine at one of the mindfulness studios came out of his session one day with a glowing smile on his face. He said that when he asked the group his usual "What brings you here?" question, someone said that she was looking for deeper meaning in her life, the underlying cause of her anxiety, and a path for working with that. My colleague and I smiled at each other and whispered, "Hooray."

I would guess that roughly 95% of the people I instruct say they're interested in meditation because they want to feel calmer and less stressed out. This is a logical motivation to want to meditate, and I hope that more and more people will realize they can use meditation as one of their tools for stress. The downside of this is just that, because of the way mindfulness meditation is being promoted, their only context makes them expect a relaxation type experience, with guided visualizations and calming music. Many people who come to these yoga-type studios are surprised that they aren't invited to lie down. (Some lie down anyway.)

As businesses, the studios want people to be happy so that they keep coming back. This sets up an atmosphere where there is pressure to entertain, to please, to make sure the experience is 'pleasant.' When someone walks into one of my meditation sessions and says that they need help with their anxiety and out-of-control mind, I'm touched that they have the courage and intelligence to try something so new and unfamiliar. I want them to feel safe and cared for, and I want to help ease their suffering. But some people are surprised that meditation is not as entertaining as they expect. I often tell them about the importance of boredom in helping us begin to notice our habitual ways of filling every moment with some kind of fidgeting. One of my meditation teachers called this "cool boredom," the good kind that we need to get back in touch with ourselves.

So I think we do people a great disservice if we peddle mindfulness as just another pleasant and entertaining thing to do—another bandaid for our discomfort. I always encourage people to keep looking for what makes sense to them, whether it's a particular teacher or kind of meditation, more exercise, therapy, or a vacation. Everyone is different and some people just need to relax.

~

Meditating together has a way of equalizing people. I remember a young woman who came to one of the studios a few times. She wore the most beautiful, high-style clothing I think I have ever seen in person, and she carried herself as a somewhat aloof and confident professional. But when she was sitting there in front of me, she was just another human being, experiencing her own body and thoughts, and I was touched by how young and vulnerable she looked.

Some people are more intellectual than others, asking questions and wanting to understand the practice. Others are more experiential and interested in how it feels. Some people have had various kinds of meditation experiences, usually using an app, and many come in with no experience at all. It's commendable that they want to take the time to check it out.

Some people come in regularly and immediately fall asleep, and that's their meditation experience. They are taking the time to stop and sit still, and that's fine. Others fidget the entire time and I'm amazed and impressed that they stay. Some come because their partner or friend wants to try it, with varying results. I think of these tagalongs as the "trailing spouses," as they're referred to in academia – the noble supporters, who may or may not benefit from being there. In a hospital or assisted living setting, the caregivers arrive in that role but often realize that the practice benefits them as well.

At the same time, meditation isn't for everyone. It can actually be harmful for people with certain conditions. Someone in an extremely anxious state, or with an anxiety disorder, can panic when faced with their own frantic and painful mind. Depending on the circumstances, they may be better served by some soothing breathing, movement, relaxing visualization, or a cup of tea. Most meditation instructors I know, myself included, learn about these things the hard way.

When I ran a retreat center in Nova Scotia, I learned that sometimes the most compassionate thing to do can be to seek professional help. People have various ideas about what a Buddhist retreat center is, and it's fairly typical for some very vulnerable, and even psychotic, people to be drawn to them. The first person who taught me this was a woman who arrived out of the blue and camped out in the center's dining room, thinking we would let her stay. I quickly realized that we were not equipped to care for this person, even though in my soft heart I always wanted to believe I could help everyone. The woman was obviously distressed and out of touch with reality, and she needed help.

I didn't know what to do, so I called someone I knew who was the head of the mental health department in a hospital about an hour from the center. He told me that I couldn't help this person, that I should not feel bad about that, and that the police were trained in handling this kind of situation. It went against all of my ingrained instincts but I knew I had no choice, and when the police arrived, they were kind and skillful, and were able to take our visitor to the hospital. I had to do this one more time when a young man arrived who was off of his meds and out of his mind. I happened to know his mother, so I called her and she told me to call the police! Both of these situations were strong lessons for me in what true compassion versus "idiot compassion" means.

Trauma is another factor in considering whether or how mindfulness can be helpful. Because mindfulness encourages people to stay with their experience and sit through whatever arises, it can trigger deep wounds and end up being retraumatizing. Meditation instructors must be very sensitive to this issue and help people balance the natural difficulty of sitting with their own minds and leaving, or being too harsh on themselves and thinking they have to endure extreme pain. Meditation is intended to be gentle and kind with a light-handed, intentional precision. When in doubt, always err on the side of gentleness and suggest options like mindful walking; sitting in nature and just looking, listening, or doing nothing; reading a helpful article or book; talking to you or some other helpful person, if that's appropriate; and just remembering to breathe. It's also important to always give people the option of keeping their eyes open, as some people may feel unsafe if they are told to close their eyes.

So it's necessary to have a relatively strong, intact ego to engage in an intensive level of meditation.

In my experience, most people who come to meditate are within the "normally neurotic" range. But no matter the context–studio, law firm, hospital, Buddhist shrine room, or someone's living room–the person sitting there is a human being, and all human beings are suffering in some way.

Mindfulness meditation brings stability, clarity, and strength to our naturally intelligent minds (see contemplations below); and as we sit with whatever arises, with kindness and nonjudgment, we begin to realize that everyone has the same fear of loneliness and failure, the same longing for love and connection, the same ability to connect with their own breath and heart, and the same capacity for joy. This is what instructors can provide to people who come to meditate: not just another pleasant, temporary experience and empty promise, but respect for their human journey and confidence in their ability to live their lives with a strong back and open front, which represents the balanced qualities of strength and gentleness. Strength gives us the ability to stay with the practice, remembering what we're doing and applying a light-handed discipline to the simple technique. Gentleness is the appreciative openness and kindness we bring to all of our thoughts and emotions. This balance is the best way to be in the world.

MEDITATION INSTRUCTION
COUNTING BREATH AND OTHER SUPPORTS

Meditation techniques are tools you can use to help bring your active mind into the present moment, resting on your object of meditation. Sometimes when your mind is very agitated or dull, it can be difficult to stay with the breath, so other supports can be added to help your practice and your mind to settle. These can be used for a whole session or for any portion of it, for example, to help settle the mind at the beginning of a session, or toward the end to help focus more. With all of these, the emphasis is still on feeling of the breath coming in and out of your body. Here are just a few of many techniques you can try:

✓ Counting breaths: There are many ways to do this, but they all have the same principle of helping give the mind a little more support. The great thing about counting breaths is that it's crystal clear whether you're with it or off thinking about something else. Here are a couple of examples of how to count breaths:
   1. Silently count each cycle of breath (inhale/exhale), beginning with one and counting up to ten, then starting over. It's better to have a finite number like ten so that you

don't get into a competition with yourself. When you lose track of where you were, just start over again at one. Each time you come back, you are accomplishing the practice.
  2. Count slowly up to four (or whatever number works for you) as you inhale, pause, then count backwards from four as you exhale. Pause and repeat.

✓ Labeling your breathing:
  1. You can silently say "In" with each inhale, and "Out" with each exhale.
  2. (From Thich Nhat Hanh): As you inhale, silently say, "I am breathing in," and then "I am breathing out" as you exhale. This can help you remember your own body and presence.

✓ Focusing on the breath: Bring your attention down from your head into your body, and feel your body breathing, in and out. You can add to that the feeling of air coming into and out of your nose, resting your attention on the whole enjoyable, relaxing process of breathing. Imagine the air filling your body as you inhale, and with each exhale you can let go of thoughts, relax, and return to the next inhale.

✓ Feeling your breathing: Placing a hand on your stomach and/or chest as you breathe can help to settle an agitated mind. Bring your attention down from your busy head and rest with the soothing feeling of your body moving gently as you breathe, in and out.

✓ Meditation music: This can be helpful if you're in an office or distracting environment. Make sure the music isn't a distraction in itself, but is more natural and non-melodic. There are endless possibilities on the internet for free meditation music, so you can search around until you find one that works for you.

✓ Visual object: Gaze softly at something relatively neutral and simple, like a special rock, a candle (careful not to stare directly into the flame), a simple statue or picture. Imagine that object being a safe, peaceful place where you can rest your mind, and come back to it each time your mind wanders. Let your thoughts about the object go, and rest simply on the image.

MEDITATION INSTRUCTION
MANTRA

A mantra is a word or phrase that's repeated over and over, and during meditation practice the object of mindfulness is the word or phrase itself. A word with meaning can be used as a contemplation practice, which is what I will describe here. Other mantra practices may use words that have no conceptual meaning, such as Sanskrit syllables, where the sound has a particular quality and the repetition helps to anchor the mind. My Buddhist teacher said that the word mantra actually means "mind protection," because it replaces unhelpful thoughts with something neutral or beneficial.

This is one simple practice that works anywhere:

✓ Begin by settling your body and resting your mind on your breathing for a little while.
✓ Now, think of a word or phrase that represents something

you'd like to remember more often in your life, embody more in yourself, or aspire to. For example, you may aspire to have greater calm, strength, peace, or focus. The possibilities are endless and up to you. Take a few moments to think about this and choose your word for this contemplation.

✓ Silently repeat this word each time you breathe in. As you repeat it, think about what it means, recalling how it feels in your own experience. Contemplation practice helps us to go beyond the concept of a word to its actual meaning, the experience or quality that the word is pointing to.

✓ When your mind wanders, just return to your word, repeating it with each in-breath.

✓ When you're ready to close, breathe your word in one last time, feeling its qualities flow through your whole body. Then simply rest with that feeling, relaxing and enjoying your own presence.

✓ Notice your gentle breathing again, for as short or long a time as you want, and then get up and go about your day. If you like, you can consider this your word for the day and bring it to mind, remembering that it resides within you.

MEDITATION EXPERIENCE
WORKING WITH RESISTANCE

It's natural to feel resistance to mindfulness meditation, because it isn't entertaining in the ways we're used to. Stopping our habitual physical and mental momentum is what I call "counter-habitual," going against the stream of our endless chain reaction of thoughts, feelings, and activities. It doesn't take most people very long to realize that something different is going on, and they may run from it and continue to look for something more temporary and less "boring." But those who stick with mindfulness meditation begin to appreciate the helpful message that resistance is bringing. It's when things get "boring" that the practice is actually starting to work.

Resistance can make us feel like we're two people—one who knows that something is good for us, and the other one who's trying to talk us out of it. So the first point about working with resistance is to identify it and remind yourself of your motivation. Having some clarity about why you're doing it and what you're doing is essential. But that often isn't enough to get us to step out of the strong current of our mental and physical habits.

Gentleness and a sense of humor are key when we feel resistance to the refreshing but unfamiliar boredom of mindfulness meditation. It's counter-productive to be heavy-handed with ourselves, because we'll soon lose our appreciation of the peace and insight that more balanced meditation will bring and our resistance will increase. The idea of exertion in mindfulness teachings is the opposite of drudgery; that is, appreciation, even enjoyment, is key to benefitting from mindfulness practice. So being nonjudgmental and kind to ourselves can help loosen the grip of resistance, and we begin to realize that no one is making us do this, it's up to us, and we love it! Discipline is light-handed and gentle, even while being precise and intentional. This includes being kind to ourselves when we buy into our resistance and talk ourselves out of the meditation session. That's okay, and you can start again with the next one.

So it's good to make your meditation session inviting, almost like you're trying to persuade a child to do something unfamiliar. Put it on your calendar like it's a meeting or a date. Make the place where you meditate as peaceful, uncluttered, and accessible as possible, so that you don't have an additional blockage of having to rearrange and fuss with things every time you want to sit. You can take your coffee or tea with you if that helps, light a stick of incense, ring a gong to begin and end, play non-intrusive meditation music, or use a guided App–whatever helps you without interfering with the basic meditation practice. You can even reward yourself in some foolish way, like putting a dollar in a jar every time you sit and then treating yourself to something. It doesn't really matter, because once you are on the cushion it's just you and your mind, your breath, and your thoughts.

Another important instruction from the Buddhist tradition is that it's better to do short sessions more frequently than longer ones less often, because long sessions will tire you out and make you less keen to do the next one. With short sessions, you can get up feeling good and you will be more likely to look forward to doing it again.

My meditation teacher once said that the closer you get to the cushion, the less resistance you will have. So, when it's time to meditate and you start telling yourself about all of the urgent things you have to do this very minute, you can notice that and take the first step toward your intended session: stop what you're doing in a way that works for you, get your water or tea, walk to your meditation place, light your incense or candle, sit down, breathe, pause and appreciate what you're doing and what you intend to do in the session, and begin. This is actually very great advice. And each time you feel resistance during a meditation session, you can notice it nonjudgmentally, pause and check in with your posture and body, sit up, relax, and start fresh. The more you meditate and become familiar with this, the more you can recognize it as just another kind of thought process and its power will diminish. It's the same as shifting any deeply ingrained habit, where you need a balance of clear motivation, discipline, and kindness, including kindness when you fail. You can learn to regard failure more as a reminder, or stepping stone, than as a problem.

Many years ago, when I was doing my first month-long meditation retreat, one of the instructors gave a short talk about resistance. I don't remember much of what he said, but he was funny and helped us realize that it was normal and we were all in the same boat, and that we could just sit with it like anything else. Mainly, he talked about how it was a sign that something interesting was finally happening, even though it wasn't interesting in a familiar way. And I've always remembered that he ended his talk by saying, with a smile, "Vive la résistance!" It's a message from the awake world.

THE SCIENCE OF
MINDFULNESS

W e're in the middle of a paradigm shift in the way meditation is viewed in the west, and we have our meditator-scientists to thank for it. These intelligent people who experienced the benefits of meditation themselves began testing it in controlled environments and finding ways to measure its effects. The results have been instrumental in validating ages-old teachings and creating a modern context and language for this way of working with our minds.

Not even thirty years ago, scientists and meditators regarded each other with skepticism bordering on disdain. From a western scientific point of view, meditation was "eastern." Its roots were religious, and its reported, subjective effects were not measurable and were therefore considered unreliable at best, since western science is based on objective, reproducible data. The overall institutional view was that meditation is a placebo and that meditators are gullible followers of charismatic charlatans.

Meditators, on the other hand, were usually people who were open to the idea that there was more to human experience than could be measured with current available tools. They also tended to be people who were dissatisfied with the status quo and were open to experimentation. Many of them were, indeed, gullible followers of charismatic charlatans. But there were also many genuine teachers arriving in the west for the first time, and the 1970s and 80s brought a flourishing of eastern traditions to Europe and North America. In addition to meditation teachers, experts in practices like yoga, acupuncture, ikebana, feng shui, various martial arts, and many other ancient eastern disciplines arrived and started inviting students.

The problem was that meditation didn't fit into our western medical tradition, which focuses on treating the physical body: bones, organs, and other biological systems. It is an allopathic system, using drugs and surgery to combat injuries and diseases of the physical body. The mind and body are regarded as separate, whereas the eastern medical system relies more strongly on what's called the subtle energy, or *chi*, that flows through the mind and body of all living things. It's the basis of the entire spectrum of life, including thoughts and emotions, and its balance or imbalance is inseparable from our emotional and physical health. In many eastern languages, in fact, there is one word for *mind* and *heart*, or mind/heart, pointing to an integration of intellect and feeling/experience. My Tibetan Buddhist teachers would naturally gesture to the center of their chests when talking about *mind*. In this world view, the mind is much more than the physical brain. It encompasses the whole universe of our experience, and as such it is incorrect to reduce life to measurable physical matter.

One of the most important pioneers in bridging this conceptual and cultural gap is Jon Kabat-Zinn, a molecular biologist who created the Stress Reduction Clinic and the Center for Mindfulness in Medicine, Health Care, and Society at the University of Massachusetts Medical School. Dr. Kabat-Zinn's seminal book, *Full Catastrophe Living* (first published in 1990, revised 2013) is a brilliant and essential textbook for today's mindfulness meditation teachers and practitioners. The crux of why Kabat-Zinn's work is so significant is that he is genuinely experienced in both meditation and science, so he understands the experiential, humanly spiritual aspects of meditation and isn't afraid to talk about them. He is respected and credible in both worlds.

Here is an example of how he explains the effect of mindfulness meditation:

> *Cultivating mindfulness can lead to the discovery of deep realms of well-being, calmness, clarity, and insight within yourself. It is as if you were to come upon a new territory, previously unknown to you or only vaguely suspected, which contains a veritable wellspring of positive energy for self-understanding and healing. Moreover, it is easy to familiarize yourself with this territory and learn to inhabit it more frequently. The path to it in any moment lies no further than your own body and mind and your own breathing. This domain of pure being, of wakefulness, is always accessible to you. It is always here, independent of your problems. Whether you are facing heart disease or cancer or pain or just a very stressful life, its energies can be of great value to you.* (Full Catastrophe Living, 2013, p. *lxi*)

Although Kabat-Zinn studied meditation with several Buddhist teachers, his interest has always been more focused on understanding and applying those principles in a western secular context. In 1979 he founded the Stress Reduction Clinic at the University of Massachusetts Medical School, where he adapted the Buddhist teachings on mindfulness and developed the Stress Reduction and Relaxation Program, an eight-week course that later came to be well-known as Mindfulness-Based Stress Reduction (MBSR). One of the important practices he developed is called the Body Scan. (See below.) Dr. Kabat-Zinn continues to be a leading teacher and voice in the mindfulness movement.

Interest in the interface between science and Buddhism was given a more international forum by the Dalai Lama, the exiled spiritual and political leader of Tibet. His lifelong interest in science led him to connect with some western scientists who had been studying with Buddhist teachers, and who shared the view that science and Buddhism are not contradictory but are based on a common principle of observation, in-depth inquiry, and analysis. The first Mind and Life Conference was held in Daramsala, India in 1987, and it became the seed for a transformative inter-disciplinary, cross-cultural dialogue that has inspired more than two dozen subsequent conferences and countless books, papers, and related dialogues. The Mind & Life Institute was founded in 1991 to provide a context within which scholars and scientists from different disciplines around the world can incorporate contemplative practices into various fields of study. Mind & Life unifies and catalyzes this community by funding research projects and think tanks, and by convening academic conferences and dialogues with the Dalai Lama. This is how the Mind & Life Institute website describes its mission:

> *Mind & Life emerged in 1987 from a meeting of three visionaries: Tenzin Gyatso, the 14th Dalai Lama — the spiritual leader of the Tibetan people and a global advocate for compassion; Adam Engle, a lawyer and entrepreneur; and Francisco Varela, a neuroscientist. While the trio understood that science had become the dominant framework for investigating the nature of reality — and the modern source for knowledge that could help improve the lives of humans and the planet — the three regarded this approach as incomplete. Whereas science relies on empiricism, technology, "objective" observation, and analysis, the Dalai Lama, Engle, and Varela were convinced that well-refined contemplative practices and introspective methods could, and should, be used as equal instruments of investigation — instruments that would not only make science itself more humane but also ensure its conclusions were far-reaching. The Mind & Life Institute was formed to bridge this divide and advance progress in human well-being.*

~

Dr. Sara Lazar reluctantly started practicing yoga and meditation when she was having trouble recovering from a running injury. She was only interested in healing her physical injuries, so after a couple of weeks of yoga classes she was surprised to find herself feeling, in her words, "calmer, better able to handle difficult situations, and more open-hearted and able to see things from another person's point of view." She was so interested in what was causing this unexpected shift that she switched disciplines from microbiology to neuroscience research and began studying changes in the brain caused by meditation. This concept is called *neuroplasticity*, the ability of our brains to change when we engage in different behaviors. These changes can be detected using MRI technology (Magnetic Resonance Imaging).

In one of her most well-known studies, Dr. Lazar used MRI to measure changes in her subjects after they meditated 30-40 minutes every day for eight weeks. It's important to point out that they were doing mindfulness meditation, not just a relaxation technique, because it's the repetitive behavior of repeatedly bringing your attention back to a specific focus that so powerfully affects the structure of the brain. In a wonderful TED talk you can find on YouTube, Lazar concludes by saying, "So the idea I'd like to share with you today is that meditation can literally change your brain."

What she found in this and other studies is that meditators have more gray matter in their pre-frontal cortex, specifically in the areas responsible for memory and decision-making. One especially striking finding was that the brains of 50-year-old meditators had the same amount of gray matter in these areas as in 25-year-olds, unlike the brains of non-meditators whose brains naturally lose mass over time. A related study at UCLA found similar significant differences between the brains of meditators and non-meditators. In this UCLA study, the brains of long-term meditators were found to be 7.5 years younger at age 50, on average, than the brains of non-meditators, suggesting that meditation may slow the aging process of the brain.

Another of Lazar and others' findings is that the gray matter in the amygdala is reduced as a result of mindfulness meditation, corresponding with subjects' experience of a reduction in stress. The amygdala is responsible for our fight, flight, or freeze response and emotions associated with fear. With no change in environmental factors, the reduced stress response reported by meditators was reflected in the neurobiological alteration of the amygdala.

Lazar has done many studies over the years that show that the changes observed in areas of the brain correspond with subjective reports of meditators, like decreased stress, lessening of symptoms associated with depression, anxiety, pain, and insomnia, and an enhanced ability to pay attention, to name a few.

~

The final scientist I'll mention is Richie Davidson, who is a doctor of Psychology, Psychopathology, and Psychophysiology, best known for his important work studying emotions and the brain. In one well-known experiment, he studied the brain of Matthieu Ricard, a French scientist, photographer, and writer who became a Tibetan Buddhist monk many years ago and lives in Nepal. Davidson wanted to see how meditation, and in particular compassion meditation, affected the brain of someone who had spent many thousands of hours meditating.

You can find pictures of Matthieu Ricard meditating with 256 sensors stuck to his head, dressed as always in his monk's robes. The scans showed that Ricard's brain produced a level of gamma waves—those linked to consciousness, attention, learning, and memory—never reported before in the neuroscience literature, according to Davidson. The scans also showed above-normal activity in Ricard's left prefrontal cortex compared to the right, giving him what Davidson called an abnormally large capacity for happiness and a reduced tendency toward negativity. Ricard thus gained the sensationalized title of "happiest man in the world."

Davidson has published many studies and books related to what he calls the "science of the mind." He has studied the brains of many meditators and found striking results not only in long-term practitioners but in subjects engaging in a three-week, 20-minutes-a-day program. In comparing the effect of mindfulness meditation on the brain to the way physical exercise alters our muscle structure, Davidson says, "It's a wonderful area of research because it shows that meditation is not just blissing out under a mango tree but it completely changes your brain and therefore changes what you are."

~

While there are still skeptics and deniers on both sides, great advances are being made toward understanding the "science of meditation." Many fields are developing which emphasize positive psychology, which has to do with analyzing, tending to and supporting mental health and well-being rather than just trying to deal with problems after they arise. Mindfulness is a natural and important component of this new, more holistic view of ourselves as human beings.

MEDITATION INSTRUCTION
BODY SCAN

In the body scan, we intentionally, mindfully bring our attention to all of the different parts of ourselves, one at a time. Mindfulness doesn't just mean a detached, clinical kind of observation, but it also involves qualities of interest, care, curiosity, and nonjudgment. So in doing this practice, we are, in effect, putting our minds into our bodies, or joining mind and body, rather than just thinking about or analyzing our bodies. We may notice pain that was previously in the background, we may feel pain more acutely, and we may feel pain without having to elaborate on and react to it emotionally. Overall, there is an increased ability to abide with the pain rather than being caught up in it. This contributes greatly to our overall sense of health, well-being, awareness, and appreciation of life.

The full version of the body scan is done lying down and can take 45 minutes or more. Jon Kabat-Zinn developed this method, and the Mindfulness Based Stress Reduction (MBSR) course still requires participants to do this long version regularly for four weeks as a foundation for further training in mindfulness.

Other versions can be as short as a few seconds or anything in between, and while most often done lying down, body scans are important and effective in sitting meditation and in our everyday lives. I will offer a version here that I use in most of my 30-minute and hour-long guided mindfulness sessions, in which you are bringing your attention to different parts of your body and intentionally relaxing and letting go of tensions you may feel in each part. This can be done as quickly or as slowly as seems appropriate, adding or reducing the parts of the body mentioned. If you have more time, you can also add a breathing component, where you inhale into each part, imagining the good oxygen and energy coming to that part and helping it to heal and relax as you continue to breathe. You can also label the sensations you feel in each part, such as a dull ache, sharp pain, tingling sensation, pulsing, flexible, light, etc.

SIMPLE BODY SCAN
(Pause after each instruction.)

Rest in an upright or lying down position, and feel where your body is making contact with your cushion, chair, or other support. Close your eyes if you're comfortable doing that, or leave them slightly open with a soft downward gaze. Take a few slow, gentle breaths, feeling your whole body receive and exhale the air.

Now, bring your attention to your eyes, noticing how they feel. Let the muscles in and around your eyes relax, as well as your eyebrows, the space between your eyebrows, and your forehead. Now bring your attention to your mouth, noticing how it feels; relax your lips, your tongue, your jaw.

(Continue this pattern, through shoulders/shoulder blades, arms, hands/fingers, back, seat, abdomen, upper legs/lower legs/, ankles, feet/toes, stomach, and chest.) Feel your awareness filling your entire body, head to toe, front and back, as you sit here right now, breathing.

~

You can do this in whatever order makes sense to you, starting, for example, with the feet and coming up the body. If you are doing this in the context of a mindfulness meditation session (I do it near the beginning of a session), you can also check in briefly each time you notice that your mind has wandered and you come back to where you are. At that point, check over your body briefly to see if your posture has slumped in some way, or if you've habitually tensed up somewhere. Then just gently sit up, relax, and start fresh.

PART TWO

Urban Mindfulness

MINDFULNESS
STUDIOS

The new concept of "mindfulness studios" was unfamiliar to me when I arrived in DC, and I didn't know what to expect. Even though I had heard of a studio in New York City through the meditation beehive, I didn't really know what these studios were or how they taught meditation. So on that strange morning when I googled "meditation jobs dc" on a whim, I had no idea what I was about to embark on in this new entrepreneurial world of mindfulness studios.

My first job interview, which to my dismay was called an audition, was with a brand-new studio a block from the White House. It hadn't even formally opened yet and the owner was still putting the finishing touches on its decor. There were three of us interviewing together that day, each giving a 15-minute meditation instruction for evaluation by the general manager. I did it in my usual traditional way, presenting the view, or reasoning for this kind of meditation (mindfulness-awareness), then leading people through the instructions on posture, breath, and working with thoughts. We then sat in silence for the remainder of the time, with a few minutes for questions at the end. The other instructors were quite different, talking through all of their 15 minute slots. We were all hired. I discovered on the website that I knew two other instructors who were already on board, both of whom had received their training in the formal Buddhist tradition that I was a part of. I had known them for many years, and this reconnection proved to be a huge help for me in navigating the strange new world of DC meditation.

My next interview/audition was with the owner of another not-yet-opened studio in Bethesda, MD. She sat nobly through my many minutes of silence, loving the instruction and suggesting I may want to talk a little more during my sessions. When her studio finally opened, I made an effort to sit in on some of the other instructors' sessions. I was genuinely curious about how they did it, and I learned a lot about what I wanted and didn't want to do. But I became much more open-minded as I realized that there was something good in all of them, and that they were genuinely helping people.

I ended up going through an incredible learning experience over the next year or so as I taught meditation in these two studios, in another one that opened a little later, and in some other places that popped up. Even though I have a lot of experience teaching meditation in both spiritual and secular environments, I found myself struggling in this new context. It seemed that anyone who had ever done a little yoga was now able to be a meditation instructor, which went against everything I had experienced in my previous training. It felt like a dream-come-true and my worst nightmare at the same time: What could be better than meditation being accepted in our culture? What could be worse than having it be watered down, misunderstood, and co-opted for profit?

~

My first "live" session was in the studio by the White House. The studio model is similar to a gym, where people can buy different membership or drop-in packages, or just pay as they go. This particular studio is trying to market not only meditation but also napping, a trend that is popular in Japan. The floor is covered with artificial grass carpeting, and the walls include some real wood and plants. It's one windowless room with curtains on tracks to provide privacy during the napping sessions.

The meditation sessions I led were 30 minutes long, and most of the people who dropped in were professionals trying meditation for the first time. Very quickly the owner realized that the offerings needed to be juicier–what I would call more entertaining–so now there are instructors offering gong and sound bathing, yoga nidra (sleep yoga), mantra sessions, and something called "de-stress." They still offer mindfulness meditation sessions and I don't know how it's all going for them. I left after a couple of months when I discovered that I was only paid half my rate unless there were a certain minimum number of people in a session, and that the owner was expecting me to provide marketing for my own sessions. For a brand-new concept in a tough market, I felt unable to afford to work downtown for this amount or to add marketing to my workload, and I departed in a friendly way.

During this time, I gave meditation instruction in the way I had been taught, with quite a lot of silence. However, with the short 30-minute sessions I made sure to have time at the beginning to ask and answer questions and explain the technique (which is done in sections with space in between), and I also left time at the end for questions and comments. People closed their eyes no matter what I said about both open and closed options (my training and practice has always been with eyes open). Occasionally someone would want to lie down, which I said was okay. They came with the idea that the purpose of meditation was to relax. I felt touched as always by people's stress and exhaustion and their need to rest, and I always tried to help them feel safe and unjudged. Especially in this intelligent and high-stress city, the people who come into these studios searching for help appear to me like souls who are washed up onto the beach by a tsunami. Most of them just need to rest; they often fall asleep.

~

The studio in Bethesda had a different decor and vision from the one downtown. The owner, also embarking on this as an entrepreneurial venture, was determined to limit her offerings to meditation. She often said that she didn't want to include anything "woo-woo," and I appreciated her vision and determination. Like the first studio, she was anticipating opening her doors and having people flood in. This expectation was based on the perceived success of studios in Los Angeles and New York who were leading this new trend. We realized after a while that the popularity of these ventures was partly due to the difference in our urban cultures, partly because they didn't hesitate to incorporate the "woo-woo," and who knows what else (personnel, location, decor, marketing, connections...).

The Bethesda studio had two fairly large group meditation rooms and two small rooms for individual instruction or private meditation. The two instructor friends I already knew also signed on to teach at this studio after I told them about it, and I started to realize that there was a sort of network of meditation teachers who criss-cross around the area and share information and opportunities. I've made some enduring friendships through this network.

The sessions here were scheduled for 30 and 45 minutes. People began to straggle in, finding us through internet searches or by noticing the sign. This studio was located right in downtown Bethesda, which has a dense population of people living in condos or working in the many private and government agencies in the area. Most of the clientele hadn't meditated before and named stress as their main motivator.

One unfortunate accoutrement of this studio was the owner's choice of meditation cushions. As always, people were offered a choice of cushions or chairs. These cushions, however, were like soft chairs with no legs, just a seat on the floor with an adjustable back. It was almost impossible to sit up straight in these floor seats, and for many they encouraged lounging and sleeping.

There was one man, a very stressed out single father, who came almost every day and slept through most of the sessions. It bothered him but I encouraged him to relax and accept whatever happened in the session. Many times he was the only person attending, so it was a little weird for me to figure out what to do with him. We tried various things, including walking meditation, but it was obvious that what he really needed was some sleep and a lot of kindness.

There were a few other men who tagged along with their more enthusiastic and experienced wives, and invariably the men–very friendly and supportive–would lean back in their meditation lounge seats and have a good nap. The gender imbalance in meditation is just cultural, and more and more people of all genders are gradually adopting this very basic and important discipline.

The light in this studio was dim. One of the larger meditation rooms had no windows, and the other one only had two that faced the side of a building that was only a few feet away. All of the walls were gray, the meditation seats were upholstered in gray, and the floor was dark brown. While the owner intended this to be both stylish and soothing, I found it depressing and not conducive to wakefulness. But this is really a matter of personal taste as well as one's concept about what meditation is.

This studio unfortunately closed after about a year. For various reasons, there wasn't enough business to sustain it, even though quite a few people had been able to connect with mindfulness meditation through its offerings. One woman who bought a series of monthly memberships is still a dedicated meditator, and she sent me this testimonial a few months after she first came to the studio:

> *I wanted you to know that I've officially meditated 30 days (almost) in a row. I especially like the part where I get to stop focusing on my breath and let the mind wander. And it doesn't go anywhere! It seems perfectly content to float in place. I'm beginning to sense that the regular meditation is really helping boost my productivity. I can stay on task more easily. This is cause for celebration.*

For the time being, I think that meditation is a pretty hard sell as a stand-alone discipline or self-help tool, especially in a city like Washington DC. American cities are so different from each other, with different histories and cultures. In New York and Los Angeles, for example, meditation seems to be a little more mainstream, even slightly "hip," and people may be more willing to do things that are considered "woo-woo." Washington, on the other hand, is a fairly conservative and intellectual place, not necessarily in its politics but in its corporate culture. It's regularly listed as one of the most, if not the most, workaholic city in the country in terms of average weekly work hours, average vacation days taken, and so on. The competition here for status is fierce. People don't tend to be touchy-feely, to say the least.

The studios that are still open have owners who are able to support unprofitable ventures, at least for a while, and who are willing to vary their offerings to include things like yoga, art, napping, and various workshops on- and off-site. It takes a high level of motivation for a person to make the effort to go somewhere for meditation, because its value still isn't an ordinary part of our western paradigm. When you go to a yoga studio, you feel like you're taking care of your body and helping yourself to be calmer, but with meditation, depending on the person and the instruction, this can be less clear.

Overall, I applaud these studios as being part of the colorful palette of ways people might hear about or approach meditation. The Buddhists say that there are 84,000 dharmas (which just means a lot) because there are so many different kinds of sentient beings in the universe. I always encourage people to keep looking until they find a way that is meaningful for them. So, as long as there are honest and kind intentions, we really can't have too much of a good thing. Maybe someday these studios will be as ubiquitous as yoga studios and gyms.

MEDITATION INSTRUCTION
GROUP MEDITATION

Unless you are meditating at home, it's likely that you are going to be participating and/or teaching in a group setting. This varies widely from office to office, from one hospital department to another, and in different studio settings. Here are some basic principles and benefits of group meditation:

✓ A huge benefit of group meditation is that it's easier to stick with a whole session when you're sitting with a group. Someone else is leading it, and the group energy is encouraging: "If they can do it, I can do it." We also hear what other people's experiences are like, and one thing we realize is that we aren't the only ones with busy minds and many questions and insights.

✓ Another benefit is that sitting with people naturally cultivates empathy. It's a very intimate, unusual thing to do (which is why the arrangement of the room needs to be as welcoming and safe as possible)–sitting quietly with other people, admitting that you're interested in stopping to rest and tune into your own body and breath. In conservative, workaholic places like Washington DC, it can take a lot of confidence and determination to meditate in the workplace.

✓ The arrangement of chairs or cushions can vary depending on the situation, and it's important to be sensitive to it. In offices, for example, people may be very uncomfortable sitting in a circle with no table, so sitting around a conference table works fine. In studios, it can be more relaxing to sit in rows or semi-circles, where the practitioners can look at the instructor and have some anonymity at the same time, not facing the others who are likely to be strangers. In other situations where the group is more consistent, circles can be a wonderful way of strengthening camaraderie and encouraging discussion.

✓ As an instructor, you need to keep a subtle eye on your group during the session and gauge their overall level of relaxation with the practice. It's not always possible to tell (someone who looks fidgety and uncomfortable may report on a profound and wonderful experience, for example), but staying tuned in helps you guide the group so that they have an encouraging experience.

✓ Provide some motivating information or simple teachings at the beginning of a session, reminding people why what they're doing is so beneficial. Note if someone is there for the first time and briefly re-explain the view and practice of mindfulness. Even for 'old-timers,' it's always good to hear this again. The guidance during the session will speak for itself, though, and there doesn't need to be a lot of elaboration.

✓ Encourage people to add their sessions to their calendars, just as they would include meetings. This is a basic principle for both group and individual practice, because it's all too easy to fill up those times with other things.

MEDITATION EXPERIENCE
WORKING WITH SLEEPINESS

There's no such thing as an ideal state of mind to bring to meditation, other than a willingness to sit with whatever it is, be nonjudgmental, and return to the practice–to the present moment–again and again. Sleepiness is a universal experience, and most people experience it sometimes (or often!) during meditation. Becoming more familiar with the practice of meditation helps us to experience sleepiness as just another state of mind/body. Meanwhile, how can we relate with it?

The great meditation masters have many remedies for falling asleep during meditation because it's such a common experience. Sleepiness is caused by literal tiredness, but it can also be triggered by the sudden contrast between activity and sitting still even if we're not particularly tired. Our busy, overtaxed minds sometimes just shut down rather than making the effort required to be present with our bodies and breath. Our speedy habitual minds can keep us going, seemingly perpetually, but are we really awake and aware of what we're doing?

Many people are mortified that they fall asleep during meditation; others seem to come to the studios to take a nap. But this happens in all settings, and I always reassure people that it's normal and doesn't make them bad meditators. The fact that someone is sitting there with the intention to stay through the session is at least 95% of what mindfulness meditation is. That is, as long as you notice, at some point, that you were sleeping, and come back to your present breathing, you are noticing what's going on and remaining on your seat. You are training yourself to notice the difference between being present and being mentally absent.

The traditional way this obstacle of sleepiness is expressed is as a mental state of dullness, which includes drowsiness. The mind can't be bothered to stay awake without its usual fidgeting and so it lapses into a stupor. It's a kind of subliminal avoidance tactic we all experience at times. The main thing is just to stay with it, coming back to the present when it's noticed, and doing that again and again in a gentle but deliberate way. Often the drowsiness will just pass. On the other hand, I've known people to actually fall over during long meditation sessions, not waking until they hit the floor! Everyone's mind is different and some people have more trouble with sleepiness than others.

The remedies for this are mainly to just stay with it and sit through it, not judging ourselves in the same way that we don't judge our thoughts during meditation. There is an attitude of kindness and curiosity as we both experience and observe the activities of our minds and bodies. Other remedies are perhaps more practical: if the room is too hot or stuffy, open a window or otherwise cool it down; take off a layer of clothing to make yourself cooler; don't eat too much before sessions; splash cold water on your face; straighten your posture.

Another remedy is to open your eyes. My meditation training and practice has always been with open eyes, and so an instruction for sleeping is to raise or widen the gaze. Many people these days equate meditation with closing the eyes, which can be helpful for reducing distractions and encouraging relaxation. But closing your eyes has the downside of increasing the likelihood of sleeping or having your attention drift away more easily from where you are.

LAW FIRMS AND OTHER CORPORATE SETTINGS

A couple of months into my urban adventure, I was contacted by a company that brings meditation into corporate settings. Based in New York and Los Angeles, they were just beginning to expand into the DC area and found me on LinkedIn. They were interested in me because of my combination of meditation and legal credentials, and after a preliminary phone call they invited me to audition with them.

Unlike the studio models, this organization contracts with large companies like multi-national law firms, commercial real estate companies, and others, to provide on-site weekly meditation sessions. Companies will sign on for an initial hour-long power point presentation, followed by weekly 30-minute sessions, for anywhere from six months to a year or more. They also provide virtual sessions for areas where there are no local instructors. The Human Resources section of the client company usually oversees and coordinates the sessions, ideally keeping them on the weekly email notices or other internal communications.

This meditation company uses a set formula for its half-hour sessions and provides its instructors with a topic each week, usually with links to studies or articles. For my audition, I had to learn the formula and give the instruction (virtually) to one of their staff people in New York. Prior to that, they required me to meet up with another woman in the area who was going to audition, so that we could practice the formula together and give each other feedback.

The formula was very specific, starting with a brief explanation of mindfulness (basically being both ancient, or authentic, and at the same time up-to-date and scientific). There would be a weekly topic about how meditation affects the brain, body, and/or experience, the meditation instruction, a body scan, guided meditation, and something inspirational to close. I found the format helpful, although when I saw mostly the same people for months I was able to extend the length of the actual meditation periods as well as the silence within those periods.

The main flaw I see in the corporate situation is the non-participation of the leadership. In the law firms I visited, for example, a few younger lawyers participated, but the majority of people were in staff positions. Even the head of HR, who was my contact person, rarely came to the sessions. Lawyers have their billable hours, which creates the perception that non-billable activities are a nonproductive use of time. I asked one young lawyer how he managed to make it to the sessions in light of this, and he shrugged and said that he just arrives at work half an hour early on the days we meditate. He also said that he experienced reduced stress and a more relaxed focus in his work, so he felt meditation was helping him to be more productive, not less. (The problem with this logic, though, is that billable time doesn't necessary correlate with productivity!)

Without participation from the top on down, ventures like these lack energy and are more of a bandaid than a cultural transformation. Companies have money in their budgets for staff enrichment, and it's important for them to show they are doing things to support the health and well-being of their people. But when the top executives and managers model being too busy to participate, lower-level staff have to be extraordinarily self-motivated and already somewhat "sold" on the idea. People who aren't familiar with meditation aren't likely to give it a try when it doesn't appear to be important to their superiors. The Mindful Leadership movement works with corporate leaders to bring about more systemic cultural change within the work environment and systems, and hopefully more and more business leaders will see the value of this for themselves, their employees, the work culture, and for overall creativity and productivity.

Another cultural obstacle in law firms, especially, is the cultural divide between lawyers and staff, and between partners and non-partners. Even in other corporate settings in DC, people who come to meditate don't necessarily know each other and can feel awkward meeting in such a different context. So these sessions tend to be quieter than those in other settings, at least initially, with people relaxing over time as they begin to feel more comfortable.

~

Being in the legal profession has particular health dangers because of the level and type of stress. Suicide rates for lawyers are recorded at up to seven times higher than the national average, substance abuse twice as high, and depression more than three times higher.

One lawyer who spent eighteen months in a POW camp and was tortured said that the nature of stress at a law firm is worse than being a POW. "At least there you can look forward to being rescued and a better life. At least there you are locked up with people who are your friends. At least there you know who your enemies are. Even some of the guards were nicer than the people in this law firm. At least there you do not have to look forward to your wife divorcing you because she never sees you." (https://www.bcgsearch.com/article/900044981/Seven-Reasons-Why-Practicing-Law-is-More-Stressful-than-Spending-18-Months-in-a-POW-Camp/) Litigators constantly navigate the uncertainty of other people's opinions and decisions, risking anger and worse from clients, competing associates, supervising partners, the courts, and the opposing counsel. There is virtually no one on the lawyer's side, and the feedback received is overwhelmingly negative, including the lawyer's own self-criticism.

I led a meditation session at a law firm in DC that was still in the aftershock of a partner jumping from an upper floor window. The people sitting around the conference room table had a softness, a bond, that was different from the typical law firm meditation group. But this was just a one-off session for an employee care week, and I never saw them again.

The cultural shift in the way we value money and status vs. intangibles like happiness and well-being has a long way to go. Not long ago there was an article in the *Washington Post* citing statistics showing that Washington is the city with the most unused vacation time. The competition here is fierce, and the "What do you do?" question is often the first box checked in a conversation to find out where someone is on the conceptual ranking scale. Your job title, salary, house, car, education credentials, memberships, bank accounts, and social and professional networks can make you appear as one thing or another in the estimation of others. I have an acquaintance who unfailingly replies to other people's news and info with stories about her connection to so-and-so who knew so-and-so important person, demonstrating this cultural need to one-up or at least be as good as, based only on the illusion of status. This kind of struggle creates ongoing stress and unhappiness.

How can we operate within this structure while maintaining our health and sense of well-being? First, it's important to be able to step back and evaluate our livelihood situations, which are unique for each of us. I know a young married couple who are both successful lawyers, having graduated from prestigious law schools and landing high-paying jobs at the Justice Department in DC after law school. One of them is still there, and the other one made the personal decision a few years ago to move into a non-profit job. Many others move out of law completely, finding the culture incompatible with their preferred lifestyle. Different things work for each of us, so it's important to look creatively at whatever box we find ourselves in.

And within any job, we can become more aware of our work habits and easily incorporate some mindfulness strategies that benefit our overall mental and physical health. Since mindfulness means noticing what's going on in the present moment, anything we can do to awaken ourselves out of our automatic mode helps to improve our mood and our effectiveness. Being at the mercy of our habitual, subconscious rumination and reactions is a recipe for anxiety, stress, depression, and other negative emotions. On the other hand, being aware that we're anxious, stressed, depressed, etc., empowers us to respond rather than react to how things are affecting us.

Someone who regularly attends one of my weekly corporate sessions expressed how meditation is helping her: "Meditation helps me in multiple ways. Immediately after leaving meditation, I feel calmer, clearer, more centered, more focused, so that I can get right back into work and be more productive than I was before, when my mind was wandering and racing. And then also, beyond just the work setting and Wednesday sessions, I try to practice a lot of these concepts of mindfulness, and walking meditation, and I find that I am more centered and more aware–probably a little more alert, even–and it's helped me in my consciousness and I think even my interactions with people, and with nature, and in my activities. So it's something I'm going to stick to. So thank you!"

MEDITATION INSTRUCTION
DAILY WORK HABITS

Here are a few simple things you can do to strengthen your ability to shift out of automatic and be more present, focused, effective, and relaxed at work:

✓ Give yourself mini-mindfulness breaks during the day. (See the S.O.S. practice at the end of this chapter.)

✓ Spend a few minutes at the beginning of the day organizing your work plan and space. It's important not to let your emails drive you, because this is both inefficient and stressful. Turn off notifications when possible, and take charge of what you choose to focus on.

✓ Take a little time to greet co-workers when you come in, actually taking an interest in them. This is not a waste of time; on the contrary, it makes for better and more creative working relationships and a more sane, civil, and enjoyable environment.

✓ Your phone can be a mindfulness reminder. Whenever it rings, pause instead of instantly picking it up, listen to the ring, take a breath, and then answer it. This will improve your ability to be more present and effective, having taken a step out of whatever mental chatter and rumination you were immersed in when the phone rang.

✓ Regularly stop to stretch, walk around, or simply look out of a window. Looking at the sky is especially helpful for opening out of conceptual ruts and expanding your awareness. Even very short breaks like these are immensely helpful, both emotionally and neurologically.

✓ When you're walking before or after work, or during a longer break, turn your attention outward to the sounds around you. Whenever you notice that you've slipped back into thoughts, just shift back to listening.

I find it easy and helpful to sit on my bed and breathe for a few minutes before lying down to sleep, or sitting in the morning before starting the day. If your workplace has any private space, you can go there, "stepping out of the stream" for a few minutes. The point is to find a time that works for you–a time to breathe and reset your brain. It will benefit you and those you interact with in so many ways.

The trick is to remember to do these things, so incorporating some kind of regular meditation sessions into your schedule is an important support. If you can find a weekly group or suggest that your company start one in your workplace, that is a convenient way to add this to your calendar. It's important to have some time with an instructor and the support of someone else leading the session so that you become familiar with how to do it yourself.

A woman who worked at the State Department came to sessions regularly at one of the studios, and she told me that it made her feel better just knowing she had it on her schedule twice a week. Another woman, an engineer in a DC consulting firm, sent me this encouraging testimonial: "Meditation has become something I look forward to every week. Pausing every Wednesday at lunch for just a 30-minute session allows me to refocus all of my energy and take a step back from the hectic work week. I'm so grateful for this practice."

It's also possible to engage an instructor for private sessions, either in your home or at your office. If you have the means to do this, it's a great way to ensure that you keep to your intention to meditate. And the one-on-one instruction can be a big support as you start to experience the effects of mindfulness practice and the way it develops for you.

~

I recently led a one-off session for a company in DC as the opening of their "Employee Appreciation Week." Some people commented afterwards that they learned more about each other in that session than they had in working together for months or years, even though we spent most of the 40 minutes in relative silence. A very large up-and-coming fresh food chain hired me to do a session in a fancy spa outside of DC as part of their conference closing. These are just a couple of examples of the many options available to help hard-working people nurture their own mental and physical health in this holistic, simple way.

Finally, I want to recommend a book called *Becoming a Joyful Lawyer* by Deborah Calloway (2012). There are many books and articles about mindfulness for lawyers and how to better manage the stress inherent in the legal culture, but this one has a depth that comes from Ms. Calloway's years as both a lawyer in DC and as a Buddhist practitioner. I especially appreciate her view that you don't just have to manage your stress, you can also find satisfaction, inspiration, and joy in your work and lifestyle.

MEDITATION INSTRUCTION
S.O.S.

S = STOP

When you suddenly notice that you have been caught up in thoughts, it's like waking up to where you really are. The more you practice mindfulness meditation, the more naturally this shift out of automatic will happen to you. At that point you STOP, or pause, simply noticing and appreciating this shift. You're back!

O = OBSERVE

Then, tune in to yourself. Notice your body, your breathing, your posture. What/how are you feeling? Observe without judgment, just with curiosity and care. You can pause very briefly, or take more time to inhabit your body and breathe. You can also take a few moments to notice what's going on around you: the sights, the sounds, the air temperature.

S = START FRESH

Having reminded yourself of your own living, breathing, feeling presence, go ahead and re-engage in your activities with a greater sense of awareness. The more you do this, the more natural it will become.

MEDITATION TECHNIQUE
MINDFUL MOVEMENT

When we are fully present, mindful and aware, our minds and bodies are in the same place at the same time. In other words, mindfulness isn't just about a disembodied "mind" but is a full mind-body experience. So it's important to treat our bodies well, remembering to break up our sitting with walking and stretching. Especially in office settings, it's helpful to include some kind of overall body stretch at the beginning or end of the meditation session. I prefer to do it at the end, so that the participants don't leave feeling sleepy and are reminded to care for their circulation and flexibility during the day. It's always important to remind everyone to only do these as they feel comfortable. Here's an example of this kind of routine, which is simple and only takes a minute or two:

✓ Back stretch: Lace your fingers together, turn your hands outward, and stretch your arms up over your head. Then, keeping your arms extended, bend down to each side, and then to the back.

✓ Torso twist: Placing one hand on the opposite arm of your chair (reaching across yourself), and the other arm on the back of the chair, turn your whole torso in that direction as you look back behind you.

✓ Shoulder rolls: Roll your shoulders a few times to the back, pressing your shoulder blades together, and then a few times to the front.

✓ Head rolls: Very gently around, twice in each direction.

✓ Arm circulation and wrist joints: Extend your arms out in front of you and slightly above horizontal. Hold them out as far as you can reach and rotate your wrists around a few times in each direction.

✓ Hand presses for carpel tunnel: Press the fingers of one hand down with the other hand, feeling the extension in your fingers, hand, inner wrist, and arm. Then change hands.

✓ Ankle rolls: Hold your feet off of the ground and rotate your ankles a few times in each direction. This exercise is important for circulation and helps prevent blood clots. (I first learned it on a long Air France flight!)

✓ Leg extensions: Hold your legs out straight and flex your muscles. Then move your feet toward you and away from you a few times. This engages your leg muscles and helps with circulation.

MEDITATION EXPERIENCE
WORKING WITH A FIDGETY BODY AND MIND

Most people find it difficult to sit still when they begin to learn how to meditate. Even if they appear still, they can find their busy minds to be quite a nuisance. This is all normal and is part of the learning process. That's why meditation is a practice: like everything we try to learn, we need patience and perseverance to advance along the natural path of "getting better at it."

Take learning to play the piano and imagine looking at

one for the first time. It's a total mystery! So first you sit down with a teacher, someone who can show you where to place your body, hands, and feet; who shows you the structure, or pattern, of the keyboard; who helps you connect the sounds with the structure; who teaches you about transferring written music to the keyboard; and who educates you in the history of composition and composers. Setting up regular lessons gives you a structure for your discipline, and in between you practice what the teacher has assigned. Those who have been able to stick with this, through all of the tedium and frustration, find an increasing facility as the process becomes more natural and coordinated. The ability to play the piano becomes internalized until it's hard to imagine living without a piano in one's life. Even when you aren't playing, your fingers are often moving in synch with the music going on in your mind. Instead of a duty, sitting down to play the piano becomes an integral and joyful part of your life.

There was a young professional woman who came to one of the studios almost every day, and I often had her in my sessions. She was friendly and extremely fidgety, never holding still. But she stuck with it, always expressing great appreciation for how it helped her to calm down. It was inspiring to see her change over time, as her body and even her constantly moving hands became more still. This increased stillness in her body was of course a reflection of more stillness in her mind, a developing stability that enabled her to rest more easily with her breath, more gently in the present.

One evening I commented on the change I had noticed in her meditation practice, and she told me a wonderful story about how mindfulness was benefitting her in her work. She had had a difficult phone call that week, she said, with an angry client on the line who was pushing her buttons. She said that, just as she felt herself about to lash out, she was able to notice this and pause, giving herself time to regroup and choose another response. Instead of an angry verbal retort, she calmly asked the client to repeat what she had said so that she could be sure she was hearing it correctly and be as helpful as possible. She told me that this provided space not only to herself but to the whole conversation, and the interaction was transformed into a helpful and civil one.

While we all have different tendencies–some more fidgety, some sleepy, some too tight, some too loose–we eventually experience all of these different mental states at some time or another, and there are attitudes and techniques for working with them. In the case of an overly active mind, a traditional image is that it's like a waterfall–constant, loud, and unstoppable. But it's also just one of many possible states of mind that we all experience at times, so, as always, the main point is to be gentle and notice it, letting it be and returning to our awareness of the breath again and again.

Many first-time meditators think that meditation is making their minds wilder, but all that's happening is that they are noticing it for the first time. The instruction for working with this includes relaxing and having a sense of appreciation for the awareness you have that's noticing it. In other words, although the clutter can feel a little torturous at times, it's happening in the greater space of your open awareness, like birds chattering and storm clouds rumbling in the vast open sky. Just let it flow like a river (or waterfall), make your posture more upright and relaxed, feel your body breathing, and feel the space around you. Don't worry about results; you're here, you're sitting, you're breathing. That's it.

Mindfulness Tools
for Activists

I n the spring of 2017, Washington was gearing up for a vote on the
Affordable Care Act. Republican determination to repeal the entire
bill without an alternative plan threatened health care for millions
of people, including cutting off funding to Planned Parenthood for at
least a year.

I was working at the Bethesda meditation studio when Planned
Parenthood contacted us inquiring about a private session for their
group. Staffers from around the country were flying in to Washington
to confer, lobby, and protest, and they were working around the clock
in a highly charged, high stakes situation. They were concerned about
burnout, interested in self-preservation, and cognizant of the need to
be aware and awake while they navigated through this political maze.

My studio owner asked me if I would be able to provide an hour-
long session one weekday during the lunch hour, so I planned for it
and headed downtown on a warm April day. The Planned Parenthood
group was using the ACLU headquarters on 15th Street for their
meetings and had set aside a conference room for this gathering. There
were about 25 people present; it was impressive that they were taking
this time to sit still. It felt like we were in the eye of a hurricane.

Activists are at a high risk of burnout, which can lead to
disengagement. This is so prevalent that it's considered a syndrome

that constitutes a significant and systemic obstacle to social justice movements. One of the causes of this issue is the culture within activist organizations and movements which lionizes sustained passion and effort, often discounting or even looking down on the importance of self-care. The urgency of issues can lead to feelings of guilt when any personal time is taken, so it's a matter of education in the necessity of restorative time for optimum effectiveness, the idea of "putting on your own oxygen mask first" before you can help others. This is counter-habitual and we still have a long way to go before we experience a true cultural shift.

A quote that went around the internet shortly after the 2016 election (which was incorrectly attributed to Michael Moore) provides a beautiful metaphor for how to gently sustain the strong effort that activism requires:

> *This morning I have been pondering a nearly forgotten lesson I learned in high school music. Sometimes in band or choir, music requires players or singers to hold a note longer than they actually can hold a note. In those cases, we were taught to mindfully stagger when we took a breath so the sound appeared uninterrupted. Everyone got to breathe, and the music stayed strong and vibrant. Yesterday, I read an article that suggested the administration's litany of bad executive orders (more expected on LGBTQ next week) is a way of giving us "protest fatigue" - we will literally lose our will to continue the fight in the face of the onslaught of negative action. Let's remember MUSIC. Take a breath. The rest of the chorus will sing. The rest of the band will play. Rejoin so others can breathe. Together, we can sustain a very long, beautiful song for a very, very long time. You don't have to do it all, but you must add your voice to the song. With special love to all the musicians and music teachers in my life.*
> *– Aimee Van Ausdall, Denver, CO*

We had a good, strong session that day, which included a short introduction, body scan, guided mindfulness meditation, and plenty of restorative silence. I told them a little about attention restoration theory, how the cognitive functions in the prefrontal cortex of the brain can become drained when we overtax ourselves without a break, which lessens our ability to make good decisions and find creative solutions to problems. When we have the equivalent of writer's block and feel stuck and unproductive, taking a break–"sleeping on it"–helps our brains restore themselves so that we can access and integrate more memory power and high-order thinking. Taking even short breaks where we limit sensory input, resting our minds, is an essential tool for optimal functioning.

I especially wanted to leave them with tools for going forward into the fray, something along the lines of a "Stop and Breathe" technique. I kept thinking about this as the day approached, not quite sure what was best. And then, the night before, it came to me: R.O.A.R.

The "R" is for Remember. Mindfulness meditation cultivates our ability to remember where we are and what we're doing. In other words, we become more used to being aware and appreciative of what we're doing while we're doing it, instead of talking to ourselves about what we're doing or thinking about what we'll do next, and so on. So the main trick is this first R, remembering that we're here, right now. Then we take a moment to check in with ourselves, Observing and Appreciating our own living, breathing presence, and then we Resume our activities from that more balanced perspective. This practice is described more fully at the end of the chapter.

Thich Nhat Hanh, the Vietnamese Buddhist teacher and activist who worked to end the war in Vietnam and was nominated for the Nobel Peace Prize by Dr. Martin Luther King, Jr., was an advocate for peaceful protest. He talks about burnout in his book *At Home in the World*:

[I]f we don't maintain a balance between our work and the nourishment we need, we won't be very successful. The practice of walking meditation, mindful breathing, allowing our body and mind to rest, and getting in touch with the refreshing and healing elements inside and around us is crucial for our survival.

Another pitfall for the activist is anger. Of course, intelligent anger about injustice is the inspiration and fuel for social justice movements. But ultimately what the activist is working for is justice, which is inherently peaceful in its fruitional form. Finding our own inner resources of equilibrium and peace helps us to manage the violence of the injustices we are striving to change, and in this way we can manifest our vision, walk our talk. As Thich Nhat Hanh said, "Our own life has to be our message."

MEDITATION INSTRUCTION
R.O.A.R.

✓ **Remember:** We are often lost in thought, unaware that we're actually here, right now. When we suddenly notice we've been 'somewhere else,' that's this quality of Remembering. So notice this alternation and acknowledge that you are back where you are, right here, right now. You remembered. Regular mindfulness practice helps you to Remember more often.

✓ **Observe:** At that point, pause and Observe yourself for a moment. How are you? Notice your body: your posture, any tension you may have in parts of your body, as well as other feelings in your mind and body. Are you feeling anxious, tense, happy, crazy, angry? Observe openly without judgment. Mindfulness is curious and caring.

✓ **A**ppreciate: Beyond Observing, you can Appreciate your whole being and your ability to have this kind of self-awareness and care. Tune into your breathing and take a few nice, deep breaths, Appreciating yourself as you are, where you are. Relax with a sense of your whole body, your mind, your feelings, all together right now, right here.

✓ **R**esume: Pause to look around you for a moment, listen to what's going on around you, feel the air on your skin, and then go forward into your activities with greater awareness, gentleness, and strength.

MEDITATION INSTRUCTION
CONTEMPLATING YOUR ASPIRATIONS

Contemplation practice involves using a word, or thought, as your object of meditation.

✓ Think of a word or phrase that represents something you aspire to strengthen and embody more in your life and remember more often during your day. Examples of these kinds of words, or qualities, could be things like calm, courage, strength, peace, listening, friendliness, and so on. The possibilities are endless and up to you. Choose one such word or phrase for this contemplation.

✓ Bring your attention to your body, feeling your posture, your stillness, and your breathing. Rest with that for a few moments.

✓ Now think of your word. Each time you breathe in, repeat that word to yourself. Turn your attention to the meaning of the word, not just conceptually but how it feels to you, from your own experience. Imagine that you are breathing in the essence of your word each time you inhale. When your mind wanders, just return to what you're doing, repeating your word and thinking about/feeling its meaning. Do this for a few minutes, or as long as you like.

✓ To close, repeat your word one last time, and as you breathe it in imagine its qualities filling you and becoming part of you. Rest with that for a few moments. Then, simply let it go and return your attention to your natural breathing, and end whenever you're ready.

You can contemplate anything in this way, choosing something you find inspiring or helpful. Doing this can help deepen and internalize your connection with these aspirations, going beyond a mere conceptual understanding to a true feeling for the meaning and experience. You can recall your word and its meaning during the day; you can even write it on a sticky note (or on your hand!) as a reminder.

THE IMPORTANCE OF SILENCE

The world is noisier than it used to be. Sounds of people, vehicles, Muzak, television, and gadgets bombard our ears at all hours of the day and often into the night. If we listen more closely, we may be able to hear the nearly constant hum of electricity, heaters and air conditioners, and all of the subtle ambient sounds that are new to the last century or so. Sitting in the cafe where I'm writing this, there is an orchestra of human conversation, some unidentifiable background music playing, beeps of a cellphone, thumps and dings from the cashier stations, occasional loud car or truck noises outside–the familiar medley of urban activity. Even when we take a walk in the woods, we may be listening to music or podcasts. A recent statistic about Americans says that we watch an average of a little over five hours of t.v. per day. A 2015 study by Common Sense Media found that teens spend more than one-third of their awake time using media such as on-line video or music, nearly nine hours a day on average.

We all get the idea–lots of noise, lots of distraction.

Florence Nightingale, who is regarded as the founder of modern nursing, is quoted as saying that unnecessary noise "is the most cruel abuse of care which can be inflicted on either the sick or the well." I was reminded of this recently when my mother was in the hospital, constantly disturbed by beeping machines, loud voices, and televisions. She was so exhausted by the noise that it was difficult for her to heal enough to be able to come home, and she was relieved to finally escape to her own quiet refuge and get some rest.

I was talking about the importance of silence the other day with one of my meditation clients. She thought it made a lot of sense but wondered what constitutes actual "silence." She said that her most peaceful and rejuvenating times are her early morning walks, when she tries not to listen to music but just walk, hear the birds, smell the smells, and so on. I loved her question, which made me think about what silence means.

A 2011 World Health Organization (WHO) study describes the positive side of the perception of sounds to be "...of major importance for human well-being. Communication through speech, sounds from playing children, music, natural sounds in parklands, parks and gardens are all examples of sounds essential for satisfaction in everyday life."

The WHO report goes on to describe the negative aspects of noise in great detail, defining the adverse effect of noise as "any temporary or long-term lowering of the physical, psychological or social functioning of humans or human organs." In addition to the more obvious adverse effects of noise-induced hearing impairment and interference with speech communication, environmental noise is shown to contribute to disturbance of rest and sleep; psychophysiological, mental-health and performance effects; effects on residential behavior and annoyance; and interference with intended activities.

Think about it: noise is used as a form of torture that has been documented as far back as the ancient Aztecs. In recent times, incessant music has been used to break down prisoners psychologically in situations that include the Iraq war and the Waco, Texas siege, as well as countless other situations where the intention is to erode the subjects' resistance. One of the terms for this use of music and sound is "futility music." It basically drives people crazy.

So, in some small way you might say we are torturing ourselves by not making more of an effort to include silence in our daily lives.

Our mental and physical health suffer in various ways, undermining our general sense of well-being. So what can we do about it?

Like the client's experience I mentioned above, taking walks without bringing along our electronic devices is shown to help our brains refocus and have better memory consolidation. One particularly interesting study published in the *Proceedings of the National Academy of Sciences* (http://www.pnas.org/content/112/28/8567) found that, "Participants who went on a 90-min walk through a natural environment reported lower levels of rumination and showed reduced neural activity in an area of the brain linked to risk for mental illness compared with those who walked through an urban environment. These results suggest that accessible natural areas may be vital for mental health in our rapidly urbanizing world." ("Rumination" is defined here as "repetitive thought focused on negative aspects of the self.")

There are many studies showing the benefits of immersing ourselves in nature, or even just taking time to gaze at nature from a window, if we're not able to go out. Various studies have shown the positive effect of windows in hospital rooms, for example. A 2018 study in the *International Journal of Gerontology* found that "… ICU rooms with windows are associated with shorter ICU stays than those without windows, suggesting that windows may be important in medical ICU rooms." Another related study found that patients in rooms with windows looking out on a natural scene had shorter postoperative stays, received fewer "negative evaluative comments in nurses' notes," and didn't need as much pain medication as patients whose windows faced the side of a brick building.

Similarly, there are many studies suggesting that school children benefit from having lessons in nature, or even from taking a walk outside before or between lessons. A 2018 article in the journal *Frontiers in Psychology* described studies suggesting that "spending time in relatively natural outdoor settings has a number of positive, immediate aftereffects on individuals, each of which is likely to enhance classroom engagement."

So, consciously disengaging from technology, traffic, and talking (what I've dubbed the three "T's") and experiencing the natural world, in whatever way is possible for us, brings many benefits to our brains, our bodies, and our spirits.

We can add a fourth "T" to the list: Thinking. Obviously, thinking is fundamental to our humanness, necessary for understanding our world, making decisions, creating, analyzing, and so much more. But we can be so caught up in and driven by our thoughts that it's easy to forget the intimate depths of experience we've known in moments of silence–those moments when something suddenly catches our attention and there is nothing but 'ah,' openness, complete connection. It doesn't matter what that something is: a ray of sunlight striking our face, the voice of a loved one, the smell of manure, a sharp pain. At that moment, there is no thought, no judgment, no storyline, just the pure, silent experience of That, whatever it is. We tend to remember those vivid experiences, because in those moments we feel completely and perfectly present and alive. Then our thinking mind kicks back in with its commentary, and we're back on the surface again. Deliberately creating opportunities for more peace and quiet, like walking in nature, or eating a quiet meal, or gazing out of a window, puts us in touch with our non-ruminative, non-discursive mind, which helps to reduce anxiety and increase awareness of our present situation.

Mindfulness-awareness meditation works directly with our thinking mind. In this ordinary and important practice, we set up a situation in which we simply observe our thoughts coming and going, neither pushing them away nor engaging with them. Metaphorically, we take time to step out of traffic and sit in the nourishing forest, enjoying the sounds and smells in a vivid and simple way. When we intentionally take the time to stop, breathe, observe our mind and body, and let go of our thoughts, we experience an outer and inner stillness that helps us remember where and who we are. This simple but powerful practice refocuses our attention back from our spinning-out thoughts and emotions to an experience of simple presence and engagement.

The benefits of this are countless, and are encapsulated by the meaning of some of the many Tibetan words for meditation: calm abiding, resting the mind, stabilizing the mind, strengthening the mind, getting used to what it feels like to be simply and fully present, clarity, awakened heart/mind, development of insight. From neuroscience and behavioral science perspectives, mindfulness meditation changes the size and shape of our brains in ways that increase our ability to pay attention, learn, and remember (among other things), while decreasing areas of the brain that cause stress and related health factors like high blood pressure, too much adrenalin and cortisol, insomnia, anxiety, and so on.

The last study that I'll mention is a 2013 study on mice (and an amazing parallel study on fungus) published in the journal *Brain Structure and Function* (March 2015, Volume 220, Issue 2, pp 1221–1228). The first experiment divided mice into four groups, three of which heard different kinds of sounds while the fourth remained in silence as a control group. To the researchers' surprise, the control group developed more brain cells in the hippocampus, the part of the brain associated with learning, memory, and emotional regulation. These findings support what is called attention restoration theory, where environments with lower levels of sensory input allow the brain to recover some of its cognitive abilities. In other words, when exposed to silence, the brain can restore some of what has been lost through exposure to excess noise.

The study on fungus was conducted by a middle school student who I meet with each week for a meditation session. I was talking with him about silence, gadgets, the mouse study, etc., when he amazed me by describing a similar experiment he conducted this year on fungus, entitled "The Effect of Music on Blue Oyster Mycelium Growth." When he told me that he had a similar result with his silent control group, I asked him if I could include this in my book. With the caveat that his study didn't have strict lab conditions, he kindly gave me his permission.

In a nutshell, he was interested in discovering how to maximize fungi growth because of their crucial contribution to biotechnology and the ecosystem. He tested the effects of three genres of music on the mycelium growth, with a fourth group acting as a control. Based on previous studies on music and plant growth, he expected classical music to have the greatest effect on the growth of the fungi. To his surprise, the control group, which was exposed to no audio, experienced the greatest growth. This led him to the conclusion that, with today's multi-purpose demand for mushrooms, mushroom farmers could be well-advised to grow their mushrooms "in an area with as little sound pollution as possible."

~

There is a scene I've always remembered from the Martin Scorsese film *Kundun*, which is about the life of the young Dalai Lama. This movie captures the feeling of the culture of profound silence and the intense monastic tradition that still pervaded Tibet as the Dalai Lama was growing up. In this particular scene, the teenage monk is in his formerly quiet study room in the Potala Palace in Lhasa, the capital city where he lives. Loudspeakers have been placed all over the city by the Chinese communist invaders, constantly spewing propaganda at all hours of the day and night. As the sound of a Chinese patriotic song invades the sacrosanct space where the Dalai Lama is reading, he says softly, "They have taken away our silence."

Find the silent spaces in your life. Walk in nature without technology, eat a quiet meal alone, take time to consciously pause and rest in silence (preferably while gazing from a window!). Turn your phone and other devices completely off at night.

More systemically, learn to practice mindfulness-awareness meditation. This will not only put you in touch with outer and inner silence, but it will also help you to remember to notice sound and silence during your day. It will help make it more of a habit to pause, breathe, and let your mind rest for a few moments or more. Then, you will return to work and other activities feeling a little more fresh and clear. And you will be more in touch with the silence within which all of the sounds are happening. The benefits are enormous.

If you want to explore the practice of silence further, consider group meditation sessions or retreats. You will return with a different outlook on what's going on around you, and how you interact with it. You can also consider doing a workshop on mindful speech, which includes awareness of silence.

Herman Melville said, "All profound things, and emotions of things, are preceded and attended by silence." Life is precious and profound. Let it be attended and enriched by silence.

MEDITATION INSTRUCTION
PRACTICING SILENCE

Mindfulness practices are about waking up to our mindless habits and getting us off of autopilot so that we can be more present and authentically engaged with our lives. Working with our habits of speech is a powerful way to strengthen our awareness, because we so often engage in mindless chatter or other forms of unhelpful or harmful speech.

If you are attending a group retreat, you will probably have the opportunity to experience the practice of silence. Participants are often instructed to remain silent either all of the time or during certain periods of the day. Anxiety about this is relieved by the ability to write notes or pull a meditation instructor aside if needed. But for many people, familiarity with silence breeds appreciation and even a sense of relief in the absence of the usual pressures to interact, answer questions, make witty remarks, and carry on conversations. Further, this kind of unusual silence fosters other kinds of more subtle communication, along with the most significant realization that much of our speech is unnecessary. Silence in a group setting helps us to be more aware of our habitual speech patterns and increases our comfort level with silence, even during mealtimes. It decreases our impulse to fill uncomfortable silences with chatter or gossip.

Here are a few ways that you can practice silence on your own:

✓ Make a quiet space in your home or at work where you can sit and rest from all of the external and internal noise. Silence your phone and computer, light a candle, sit comfortably, and appreciate the healing quality of this time you are giving yourself. Let your mind rest on the sensation of breathing gently and slowly as you sit on the peaceful, still earth.

✓ Take a walk without your phone and intentionally focus on the sounds around you, coming back to them when you notice yourself getting caught up in thoughts. Feel and appreciate your whole body as you walk along, step by step.

✓ Take a "noise break" during the day, even for a few minutes. Leave your technology, close your door or go to a relatively quiet place, and rest your mind on your breathing. Breathe slowly and gently, deliberately appreciating this time as a way of rebooting your over-taxed brain.

✓ Create a silent mini-retreat for yourself. You can do this even if you live with other people, if they are supportive and you can explain it to them. Just abstain from talking for a day, or half a day (unless an emergency comes up and you have to). This can help you to notice your impulse to speak impulsively and unnecessarily.

✓ Practice silence when you are doing a non-conceptual task, like housecleaning, gardening, washing the car, and the like. Set the intention to stay in the moment, letting go of planning and ruminating, and listen to the silence as you engage in your activity. When you're finished, you can acknowledge what you've done with appreciation and gratitude.

MEDITATION INSTRUCTION
MINDFUL SPEECH

The definition of mindful speech is basically speech that doesn't cause harm. Harm in this case can mean many things: confusion, anger, jealousy, strife, etc. Here are some of the ways in which you can work on strengthening mindfulness of your speech:

✓ Make a commitment to yourself not to lie. My Buddhist teacher once said that not telling the truth defeats the purpose of speech as communication. Notice your tendency to avoid the truth at times, and pause to reflect on what is causing this resistance. What are you afraid of? Like all mindfulness practices, this is not meant to be judgmental, but you can learn a lot about yourself by becoming more mindful of these patterns.

✓ Make an intention to speak kindly, even when you are angry. Harsh words hurt others and aren't all that effective. And if you're too angry to speak kindly, then just say nothing. Pause and take a breath; don't be afraid to remain silent, or walk away. This can create less harm than pouring out aggressive, hurtful words that reverberate for a long time.

✓ Make a conscious intention not to gossip. This is interesting because it always involves communication with at least one other person, and it can be a pattern with the two or more of you. So you can think of a kind way to disengage, sometimes just changing the subject, or, if necessary, saying that you don't want to talk about someone when they're not here—or whatever you think is appropriate. This is a hard one because the other person may feel offended when you do this, but they can also end up respecting you for it and following your example. You can also talk about this with your work group or community and adopt it as a group practice.

✓ Practice listening: Give someone your full attention without thinking about other things, interrupting, pre-judging, or thinking you have to know the answers. Notice their body language and tone, allow silence as part of the communication, and ask them questions to clarify or explore further.

✓ Notice your own speech patterns and see if you can change your habits a little: try to reduce filler words ("um," "like," "you know," etc.), speak a little more slowly and deliberately, be more intentional about what comes out of your mouth.

MEDITATION INSTRUCTION
MINDFUL LISTENING

This is a listening practice to do with another person, so in a group setting people can pair up. It's important to be sensitive to the comfort level of the group, and this version is the least threatening in that it doesn't require anyone to tell a personal story.

✓ Explain that each person will talk for two minutes about anything they like. It can be a personal story, what they like about their commute to work, a movie or book, anything at all. They will speak without interruption, and there will be a signal when it's time to end.

✓ Sit silently for a minute or so, giving people time to consider a topic and take some good calming breaths. Then give a signal, like a gong, for the first speaker to begin. After two minutes, give a signal to end, then a minute or so of silence, then a signal for the second speaker to begin.

✓ The speaker's instruction is to notice their own speech: choice of words, filler words, body language and eye contact, feelings and level of comfort or discomfort, relationship to silence as they're speaking, and what it feels like to have someone intentionally listening.

✓ The listener's instruction is to listen openly and attentively, noticing their own body language and eye contact, level of comfort and tendency to want to speak, tendency to be distracted by their own thoughts, to judge or have opinions.

✓ When the second speaker's time ends, sit silently for another minute. Then have a discussion about how it felt to be speakers, and how it felt to be listeners. This is likely the first time anyone has done an exercise like this, and people often have insights into their own behavior. How did you feel when speaking/listening? What did you notice about yourself/ your mind/your body? What did you find helpful about this exercise/how do you think this kind of awareness might help in your communications with others?

FAMILY MEDITATION

O n a beautiful, almost-springlike Sunday morning, I pull up to the elegant NW Washington home and notice that the storm door is propped open. I smile to myself because I interpret this as a sign of welcome anticipation for our appointment. There's no ringer on this house so I knock... and knock again... and finally just give it a good whack. That seems to work because I hear sounds of someone hurrying down the hallway, and finally a slightly breathless woman, Anika, opens the door and greets me with flustered apologies and clouds of bacon smells wafting all around her.

"Oh my gosh, we forgot about today! Please come in, would you like some tea? Noah isn't here, he had an overnight with a friend. Oh dear!" Anika's husband, Myles, joins us in the hallway, smiling a little sheepishly at having forgotten our weekly meditation date.

These two young DC professionals are successful, busy, and dedicated to their two children, age 12 and 8. They also juggle trips to see their aging parents, who live far away and are beginning to have more medical and care needs. With a full work schedule, including a lot of travel for Myles, and all of their multi-generational family responsibilities, you could say that they're a pretty typical Washington family.

Their older child, Noah, expressed interest in meditation after some sessions were offered at his school. He is an exceptional child, bright and friendly, a music student who practices his instrument an hour every day, and is well-rounded and well-spoken. At the same time, he is still a natural and tender child. His parents are very aware of the depths of the tradition of meditation and they sought out a teacher who could work with their family. While they are doing this primarily for their son, they join our sessions both to support him and to learn the skill themselves. And the benefits to their overall family culture are enormous.

"It's no problem, don't worry," I say to them, suggesting we just skip this session and meet next week. But they insist on having our session anyway, with just the three of us. So they scurry around, rearranging a space, getting their other child situated (she opts out of meditation so far, but will come in when lured by the short videos I sometimes play about how mindfulness is being taught in schools and other related topics). They are slightly mortified by the weekend state of their house, continuing to apologize for what they call a mess but what I assure them is really a very cheerful mess.

We eventually settle down—Myles and I on cushions on the floor, Anika on a chair—and arrive.

Whew.

Meditation always feels like that: "Whew, I made it!" I call that "arriving." Our lives can be so busy, in all of our different ways, that it's hard to stop our forward (and often hamster-wheel-like) momentum. Sometimes it can feel almost impossible to step out of our habitual routines of mental and physical occupation with *something*. While we all have the natural ability to deliberately focus our attention, all too often our minds lapse into what neuroscientists call our default mode, those unconscious ruts of inner dialogue, rumination, reaction, and just plain "spacing out." So spending a little time each day practicing mindfulness strengthens our ability to be present and to notice more frequently when we're not. And what could be more important than being present *in the present*, where we're actually living? Once you get this point, mindfulness practice becomes as basic and necessary as physical exercise, eating well, sleeping enough, and all of the basic skills you need to lead a conscious and full life.

For children, mindfulness practice is proving to expand social and emotional awareness and improve students' academic performance. It helps them to settle down at the beginning of the day or week, after recess, and between subjects. It is also having a significant effect on discipline issues and detention rates in schools where it is integrated into the overall culture of the school. Perhaps most importantly, helping children become familiar with the feeling of being self-contained— sitting quietly, feeling their own breathing, tuning in to how they feel, and learning acceptance of their ups and downs—empowers them to appreciate who they are, as they are. The basis of mindfulness practice is acceptance and curiosity, an alert openness that reminds us again and again that we're right here, between the earth and the sky, and that's good and fine even if we're feeling emotional. And we quickly and naturally begin to realize that we're all in the same boat, which is the basis for empathy.

The main empowerment that comes about through mindfulness practice is awareness of our habitual reactions. We begin to notice more often how something is affecting us *before* we mindlessly, automatically react to it. This gives us more agency in our lives and helps interrupt cycles of confusion or aggression, no matter our age. Teachers who can work with students from this basis realize significant shifts in the environment of their classrooms and the ability of their students to work together and feel more relaxed and happy.

Many excellent organizations are now bringing mindfulness training into schools all across the U.S. (and in other countries as well). In the Washington DC area, for example, the *Peace of Mind* organization, which began in 2003, has a wonderful three-level curriculum for children in Pre-K through Grade 5. Their model is especially sustainable because they train the teachers and other qualified educators to deliver the program, and they now have branches nation-wide. Their curriculum "gives students the tools to notice and manage their emotions, practice kindness and empathy, understand their brains, build healthy relationships and solve conflicts peacefully."

Two other organizations in the area are *Mindful Schools* and *Minds Incorporated* (now called *Minds*), which both serve children in grades K-12. All of these organizations have a wealth of experience and information, and their schools are noticing marked benefits in the students' social interactions, ability to pay attention, anger management, and readiness to learn. This is a rapidly expanding field and there is a wealth of expertise developing that will hopefully create a cultural change in the way we work with children in school settings.

There are many skillful techniques for teaching mindfulness to children and many people who have more expertise in this area than I do. I encourage those who are interested to look into the school curricula and other great resources (like Goldie Hawn's *10 Mindful Minutes* with its "MindUp" curriculum, and many others). Even very short, simple things will make a big difference for your child and your family.

MEDITATION INSTRUCTION

MINDFULNESS OF BREATHING

Mindful breathing calms our stress response, sending a signal to the brain that we're not in danger. It also helps develop self-awareness and strengthen attention. Start with just a minute or two of mindful breathing, asking the children to sit with their eyes closed or open, whichever they feel comfortable with. Starting with a resonating sound, like a chime, engages them in mindful listening and helps them to settle into silence. They will easily build up to a few minutes, with interspersed guidance during that time. They can put their hands on their bellies and feel the movement of breathing. They can feel the air coming in and out of their noses. Encourage them to relax, to bring their attention back to their breath, and to let their thoughts drift away like clouds in the open sky. Counting breaths can also give a busy mind a little more of a handle, or project, for staying with the breathing.

The practice is the same for adults, but with children it's even more important to have short sessions that they can enjoy and feel good about. In post-meditation, there are quick breathing practices they can use to help calm down, like "PBS: Pause-Breathe-Smile," or to check in with how they're feeling, like "SOS: Stop-Observe-Start Again." These are equally effective for adults, because they are great tools to help us slow down and remember where we are, and to touch in with how we are.

MINDFULNESS OF OUR SENSES

Appreciating silence helps us pay more attention to what's going on around us. Starting with a few moments of silence, ask the children to mentally identify five things they can see, trying to choose things they don't usually notice, like a shadow, a small crack, etc. Then move to feeling, bringing awareness to four places your body is feeling something, either internally (like a feeling in your throat or stomach, or a pain or itch somewhere) or where your body is making contact with itself or with the floor or furniture, or feeling a breeze or the warm sun. Next, notice three things you can hear, listening to all of the layers of sound, from obvious to subtle, near to far. Next, notice two things you can smell, trying to expand your awareness to things you don't usually notice. It doesn't matter what we think about the smell, it's still a smell! Finally, notice one thing you can taste right now, inside of your mouth, or in the air you breathe into your mouth.

You can also do a mindful eating exercise with something simple, like apple slices, raisins, or M&M's, which is always fun. After these exercises it's good to let the children (and adults) describe their experience, because everyone notices, and doesn't notice, different things—very interesting!

MINDFULNESS OF EMOTIONS

Naming how we feel can help give us more perspective and shift our internal state. So instead of just *being* anxious, for example, it's possible to step back and *notice* that we're feeling anxious. Being conscious, or mindful, of how we're feeling allows us to feel and acknowledge the emotion instead of being controlled by it. It allows us to cradle the feeling with kindness and step away from our usual cycle of reaction without trying to push the emotion away.

One way I like to do this is to ask everyone to describe how they're feeling in weather-related terms—a raw overcast day, or a beautiful sparkly spring day. This kind of contemplation helps us all expand our awareness and emotional vocabulary. And it's absolutely mind-boggling to hear the insight and creativity in people's responses. It's also interesting to close a session with the same question to see how feelings may have shifted, asking students to visualize their first image and imagine it settling down a little, or brightening up, if they can, joining it with how they feel now. Again, the point really is self-empathy, learning how to be gently and powerfully present with all of our ups and downs, not trying to reject them but developing more awareness and an ability to be present with whatever happens to be going on.

We can also mentally observe our bodies and see if we can relate our emotion to a sensation, and then try to describe it in terms of its location, how it feels, what shape it seems to have, its temperature, and so on. This is the basis for an important conversation about how our emotions affect our bodies, like when we feel butterflies in our stomachs, or a hot face, or clenched teeth.

PRACTICING KINDNESS

Self-empathy naturally expands to noticing how others are feeling. Practicing kindness is a form of mindfulness because we deliberately pay attention to others and make a conscious effort to extend ourselves in some way. It helps us to be more awake in our lives because it takes us out of our more mindless, habitual patterns. We can do this internally just by making a deliberate effort to notice people and imagine how they're feeling and what their lives may be like. This can be an exercise using pictures or talking about someone in school (or work) who is a bully, perhaps, or someone who is bullied.

Performing acts of kindness makes us feel good and helps others. Each time we remember our intention to be deliberately kind or helpful, we increase our awareness of what's going on around us as well as our feeling of empowerment that we can choose our actions. Children and adults can decide to do at least one helpful or kind thing each day, and notice how it feels. These acts can be as seemingly small as smiling at someone, holding a door, or letting someone go in front of you, up to bigger actions like talking to someone who seems alone, making food for someone, or sticking up for someone who is being bullied. These acts have powerful effects on ourselves and on everyone they ripple out to.

A couple of years ago I went to a local elementary school to observe someone from the *Minds* organization conduct a few of her weekly sessions. One of their ongoing discussions was about kindness, and the children had been consciously practicing that over the week. To illustrate what happens when someone does something unkind or mean, the instructor took a piece of paper and crumpled it up into a tight ball, and there was lots of agreement in the room that it feels like that when someone is mean. Then she talked about apologizing and trying to make amends, and everyone agreed that they should do that. To illustrate that, she uncrumpled the paper and smoothed it out. But then she said, "But see, even though the paper is better now, it isn't smooth like it was before. The unkindness has left permanent marks on it." They could see the lesson that you can't undo things you've done and pretend they never happened, so it's better to be mindful and try to catch yourself before lashing out.

CONTEMPLATING INTERCONNECTEDNESS

The Vietnamese Buddhist teacher Thich Nhat Hanh says that if you look closely, you will see a cloud floating in a sheet of paper. Without a cloud, there will be no rain to make the trees grow, and without trees, we can't make paper. Looking at objects in this way is an awareness practice, opening the mind to a larger perspective and a greater appreciation for the ordinary magic all around us. This can be a nice way for a family to start a meal together, thinking of some of the endless things that had to come together to bring the food to their plates.

MINDFUL MEALS

✓ Decide when your family can sit down and have mindful meals together. The more you do this, the more natural it will become.
✓ Take a few moments to consciously settle in your chairs, make sure everything is ready, and breathe.
✓ You can even ring a gong or bell to note the beginning of your

meal, or you can bow together, or do something else to help mark the intention to begin.

✓ Serve the food in relative silence, limiting remarks to basic issues of how much, etc.

✓ Look at your food and notice the colors, shapes, and smells. Depending on your family, this can be done silently or as a discussion. You can add something unfamiliar to taste and talk about.

✓ Then, turn to gratitude: For the cook, the shopper, the people who unloaded the trucks and put the food in the store, the farmers who grew it, the sun and rain–the list is endless.

✓ As you eat, remember to see, taste, and enjoy your food, eating a little slower than usual. If this is hard, you can try setting an ending time for your meal so everyone doesn't feel they have to rush.

✓ The gratitude practice will probably spark more conversations, so go with it. Don't force your children to eat, but you can encourage them to at least have a taste of something new. You can also share your hunger levels before you eat, during the meal, and when you're finished.

✓ Do something to mark the end of the meal, like ringing the gong or bowing again, or whatever little ritual you come up with. The point is to end together.

✓ Make clean-up part of the meal, deciding who does what. You can also have a discussion about what happens to leftover food and the endless important topics that branch off from that.

Mindfulness Jars

Mindfulness jars are pretty, captivating, and easy to make. All you need is a jar with a top, water, clear glue, and glitter. The glitter in the shaken-up jar represents our stirred up thoughts and feelings, and we can sit quietly and breathe as we watch the glitter gradually drift down to the bottom, leaving the water clear and calm. Children enjoy shaking up the jar and talking about what that represents, and the quiet they experience in watching the glitter settle helps calm their emotions and reduce feelings of stress. The more glue you add to the water, the longer the glitter will take to settle, so you can experiment and get the kind of jar you want. Glue the lid onto the jar to prevent accidents.

BREATHING ROOM

A breathing room, sometimes called a peace room, is a place in your home or school for breathing and calming down. If you don't have a whole room for this, you can make a space that's clean and simple. The idea of this room is that it's an alternative to acting out in anger, to judging yourself for your anger, or for judging others when they enter into the breathing room. Anger is a normal part of being human, but it's important not to let it affect your behavior in a harmful way.

When you feel upset, out of control, or otherwise need a peaceful place, you know that the breathing room is a safe space where no one will disturb or challenge you. It's good to have some kind of bell or gong there, so you can sit, ring the gong to acknowledge you are there, and count ten in-and-out breaths: in-out-one, in-out-two, and so on. How you breathe, and for how long, is up to you. You can also go to this place in the morning before school, when you get home, or any time. If someone is already in the room, you can join them quietly, ring the bell, and breathe.

Now back to Anika, Myles, and Noah: When I arrived at their house the next week, everyone was scrubbed and ready to go. The younger sibling reluctantly stayed for two very short videos about meditation I had selected, completely captivated for those four minutes before squiggling away again. The rest of us sat quietly for a few moments and then began by describing how we feel in weather-related language. Everyone laughed when Myles said he felt like a hurricane that isn't sure if it's going to make landfall or stay out to sea. Anika felt like a tornado, out of control with so many things to do. Noah and I both felt similar, like the foggy and slightly prickly cold weather outside.

I realized I forgot my gong, so Myles quickly found a good one on the internet and, as I led us into the meditation, I gave Noah a signal when to "ring" it. It turned out to be a beautifully sustained, minute-long series of sounds, which we all enjoyed silently.

After our simple body scan and guided meditation, I read them a passage from one of the many wonderful books about meditation, and we talked about how learning this practice is like learning any new skill. Similar to the beginning stages of playing an instrument or driving a car, mindfulness meditation requires instruction from someone who is experienced in both the theory and the practice, and then the student must practice it again and again until it becomes familiar and coordinated. The awareness practiced in formal meditation—of our bodies, of our thought processes and emotions, of where we are and what we're doing, of what's going on around us—begins to seep into our daily lives, helping us to be more conscious and engaged.

Myles asked me how he can practice this when his work doesn't seem to allow any time for meditation, especially when he's traveling. I assured him that doing our weekly sessions gives a good ground for remembering mindfulness in all kinds of situations, and we can all also benefit by pausing and noticing where we are and what we're feeling whenever we have little moments like waiting for an elevator, getting our coffee (smell the aroma, feel the heat, notice how you're feeling while you're going through the ritual), driving, opening our computer, or beginning a meal.

The essence of mindfulness is *remembering:* waking up from our habits and remembering we're here, and being curious about what's going on in that situation. And remembering our breathing, which is also happening in this present moment. We also talked a little about how he may try scheduling short daily sessions, putting them into his calendar and not worrying when they don't work out. He said that he realizes he really does have time for 5-10 minute meditation sessions and that he feels re-motivated to make more of an effort to do this.

We closed by recalling our weather systems and then contemplating them silently for a few moments to see if we still feel the same. Myles remained concerned about his hurricane but expressed appreciation for the time we had as a "calm before the storm," which helped him feel a little less tense. Anika said that her tornado had actually lost some of its steam and didn't feel quite so out of control. Noah and I both noted that our prickly dark weather had lightened up a little, which was interesting. We made plans to be in touch in the coming week because our schedules, always challenging, were presenting a couple of extra potential conflicts. We laughed and realized this was just another opportunity to pause, breathe, and smile.

~

Anika and Myles sent me this delightful message about why they value having weekly mindfulness sessions:

> We began meditation as a way to cope with daily stress, come together spiritually and connect peacefully as a family. We have realized that mindfulness doesn't promise to deliver on any of these goals, but that sitting still and centering yourself for a while brings its own joy and produces its own results.
>
> Like most families in our communities, we lead busy lives, our kids have a lot going on and on a daily level we

found ourselves pushed and pulled in many directions. Our 12-year-old was having trouble sleeping at times, we were having trouble waking up. It just felt like we all needed to find that quiet inner core that would center us. Our weeks are still rushed but having that quiet hour on the weekend together as a family with Patricia guiding us has helped tremendously.

Patricia has made the sessions a time of calm reflection and being – she brings with herself a certain peace that creates the right space for these sessions. Most sessions we discuss a thought, a written chapter or an idea and it has been a terrific conduit to having meaningful discussions with our children and bandy about some bigger ideas concerning life, the world and our place in it. Often, these are discussions that they would not be willing to sit down and have otherwise. We're not religious so for us, the practice of mindfulness seems a good way to impart a deep spirituality and respect for the world in our kids.

We would highly recommend practicing mindfulness as a family and making it the common ground to build a common worldview on.

MINDFULNESS FOR THE ELDERLY

N ot long after I moved back to the DC area, a friend of mine asked me if I would be able to take over his weekly meditation sessions at an assisted living facility. This is a challenging environment, with people in their 90s and above who have serious physical, mental, and emotional issues. Those who move there face the loss of their familiar homes and routines, and once there, the realities of sickness and death are constantly present.

Because this particular facility is part of a large hospital complex located in one of the wealthiest parts of Washington, the environment is attractive and bright, the food is good, the staff is friendly and professional, and there are a variety of activities and classes offered each day that residents can enjoy. But most interesting to me are the residents themselves, very high-powered people who have come to this place to receive the support and help they need during this stage of their lives. There are diplomats, lawyers, government officials, real estate developers, writers, musicians, academics, and more. One of the people I felt a surprising kinship with was a retired four-star general, who is, sadly, no longer able to participate in our weekly group. Renowned for his accomplishments, his eloquence, and his good heart, it was largely thanks to him that our group discovered the connection between mindfulness and poetry.

As people arrive each Wednesday afternoon–most either with walkers or pushed in wheelchairs by caregivers–we chat a little or a lot, depending on who is there and the mood of the day. We form a circle, and I often bring flowers or leaves from outside the building to place in the center, representing the season and the weather. I make a point of sitting next to those with more severe hearing loss, and I make a list of everyone present as a way of engaging them about their first and last names and their family origins.

We usually start by going around and introducing ourselves. This is an integral part of the session and can be brief or not, because it is as important as any other activities we may do. Gathering in a circle is simple, powerful, and ancient, and it creates an environment where humans can naturally meet each other as equals. Our changing societal structure has resulted in more and more isolation for individuals, and older people can become especially cut off as their spouses and friends pass away, their jobs and routines end or change, and their ability to get out on their own is reduced or impossible.

I never know what this opening conversation will bring up. Once, a resident that most people knew had died just before we met, and after a few tender comments about the person, death, and what it was like to live in that environment, we sat in silence for a long time. There were occasional tears and simple comments, and it felt like a powerful wake.

The National Academy of Sciences and others have studied the effects of isolation and loneliness on the senior population, finding it to be a significant health factor that increases the risk of mortality, negatively affects both physical and mental health, and contributes to cognitive decline and risk of dementia. It has also been shown in numerous studies that loneliness in seniors is a major risk factor for depression and high blood pressure. Even within a community setting like an assisted living establishment, individuals can experience isolation and loneliness due to the difficulties of venturing out of their rooms, of engaging in conversation or activity once out, of creating new relationships without their spouses or other more familiar social groups, and simply because they don't feel up to it. It's easy for loneliness and depression to snowball.

Sitting together in a mindfulness circle for an hour promotes connectedness. A UCLA study showed that seniors who participated in an eight-week meditation program significantly decreased rates of self-reported loneliness. Other studies, involving brain scans, show that mindfulness meditation stimulates and strengthens the area of the brain in the pre-frontal cortex associated with feelings of happiness and well-being. Millie, who was 101 years old at the time and passed away recently, articulated this in a helpful way: "It's a very unusual situation, because we have many activities here but we do them from a sense of duty, or need. But this one is purely peaceful and enjoyable, and I love coming every week."

Mindfulness is the theme in our weekly sessions. We have discussed the title of the group, which originally was something like "Weekly Meditation" and which I changed to "Mindfulness & Meditation." But after we got more into poetry, we decided to change the name to "Mindfulness & Poetry." The group wisdom of this elder generation felt that many people would think that meditation is something weird, even though those who attend understand what it means.

So here's what we do generally, not necessarily in this order:

- ✓ Gathering, greeting, introductions and check-in
- ✓ Opening aspiration
- ✓ Mindful breathing, body scan, and gentle movement
- ✓ Mindfulness meditation
- ✓ Sometimes a theme, like acts of kindness, gratitude, benefits of mindfulness to the brain, something related to the season, etc.
- ✓ Sometimes I read them a story and we talk about the meaning/ moral.

✓ Poetry
✓ Occasionally music
✓ Parting

~

Helping people to be more aware of their own **breath** as a familiar resting place for the wandering mind reduces stress and anxiety. It can be helpful to start a session with a few long breaths, in through the nose and gently puffed out of the mouth. This has a settling effect on the individuals and the group.

A simple **body scan** is always a powerful way to notice where tensions are held, by nonjudgmentally bringing our attention to all of the parts of ourselves we may forget to notice and where we may unconsciously hold tension. Relaxing these areas–like our eyes, jaw, shoulders, stomach, and so on–is beneficial to our overall health. For example, remembering to notice tension in our stomach, breathing down into it and relaxing, has been shown to help the digestive system. Our bodies reflect our minds and vice versa, so being more conscious of our bodies helps our overall health and mood.

Mindful movement is important for people with limited mobility, helping to prevent blood clots, maintain some flexibility, and improve circulation and mood. I emphasize the importance of paying attention to one's own body and only doing what feels comfortable. We do a very simple, gentle seated routine, moving through the head, shoulders, arms, wrists, legs, and feet. Sometimes I associate the movement with images from nature, imagining the wind or the trees, for example, and the feeling of dancing with our arms and bodies.

Mindfulness meditation has been shown to sharpen and focus the mind. Many studies have shown that both long- and short-term memory areas of the brain improve through this kind of meditation. People are encouraged to notice their minds wandering and come back to this present situation where they are simply sitting and breathing.

Reminders to return to the breath are interspersed with short periods of silence. Sitting together in this way is relaxing and profound, in a very simple, basic way.

Our discovery of **poetry** has been a gift in so many ways. It started when the General told us stories about his Irish mother, who sang songs and recited poetry to him as he was growing up. He told us these stories every week, usually accompanied by both tears and laughter. One of her favorites had been "Trees," by Joyce Kilmer, so I printed out some copies and brought them to our group–and our poetry took off from there. *Trees* has become our all-time favorite and we recite it almost every week. We use it as a way of visualizing the beautiful images it describes, and we also practice memorizing parts of it, since memorization strengthens the brain (especially the first verse: *I think that I shall never see/A poem lovely as a tree*–and the last verse: *Poems are made by fools like me/ But only God can make a tree.*). Sometimes we pause after each verse and rest silently with the images. And we often discuss how the poetry makes us feel. Over the months we have discovered more of Joyce Kilmer's poetry.

We now have a whole portfolio of poetry, some I have found and some suggested by the group. Reading poetry has been shown to reduce stress and improve memory. I have also noticed that it accesses a deep part of our memory that responds to cadence and imagery in an almost magical way.

A woman in our group, Carol, always attended but hardly spoke for months and usually seemed unhappy. She is unable to walk and has severe hearing loss. One day, I happened to bring in a poem from *A Child's Garden of Verses* by Robert Louis Stevenson called "The Swing." As I handed around the copies and she held hers close to her face to see it, she suddenly lit up. "I learned this poem in the third grade!" she exclaimed, and she started reciting it from memory. This sparked a lively conversation about where she was in the third grade, continuing all the way through her travels around the world with her diplomat husband and all of the places she had lived. (Her favorite place to live was Paris!) She lights up every time she sees this poem, and we all recite it enthusiastically and enjoy its swinging cadence. We also have a similar poem from the same collection called "Bed in Summer," as well as delightful poems by A.A. Milne, William Wordsworth (*I Wandered Lonely As A Cloud*), Robert Frost, and many others.

Living in an assisted living community offers many opportunities for practicing mindfulness. We often talk about cultivating our awareness of small acts of kindness, especially by noticing people who may be alone or sad and reaching out to them. We talk about the benefits of mindful eating and other ordinary activities, and the importance of staying connected with nature even from our windows. I think that one of the greatest gifts of mindfulness practice is the reminder that, no matter how difficult our thoughts, we can rest our mind on our breath, which is always here for us as long as we are alive.

For **caregivers**, it's important to stop and assess signs of burnout so that you can remain healthy. Taking time to care for your own needs as a caregiver isn't just a good thing to do, it's essential and just as important as the care you are giving to another person. Find a caregiver support group, get some regular exercise, listen to music you like, talk to a friend.

Mindfulness meditation is a simple and accessible way to remember to stop, breathe, and check in with yourself. As caregivers, we can so easily lose ourselves in the constant demands facing us, which can take a physical and emotional toll. So if you feel signs of stress and burnout like exhaustion, difficulty sleeping, persistent resentment and anger, substance abuse, depression, or other related issues, please remember the instruction we all receive on airplanes to put on our own oxygen masks first. If we can't breathe, we are useless or worse in our ability to help anyone else. We can do this, even if we're in a situation where we can't get away and have little personal time or space. The key is gentleness, to ourselves first, then to others.

Having the ability to be present with someone can be the greatest gift you can give. When you're with someone who is infirm, in pain, or experiencing dementia, mindfulness training is a great support in enabling you to be with whatever is going on with appreciation and openness, not caught in your own expectations about what should be happening. The familiarity with our own thoughts that mindfulness meditation gives us can also help us to be more aware of the kind of negativity that can add to our stress or depression, like blaming ourselves, feeling guilty or inadequate, becoming impatient, irritated, and angry, and so on.

~

One of the women in our group brought a quote she has had on her wall for many years, which I retyped and copied for everyone. This quote has become one of the important things in our repertoire, a source of inspiration and guidance:

> *If anyone were to ask me what the purpose of life is, I would say the opportunity for doing a kind thing for someone else each day... In no other way, I am convinced, can true happiness be obtained. – Eleanor Roosevelt*

This spring I walked all the way around the Tidal Basin, enjoying the crowds who were out to see the cherry blossoms on a warm Washington evening. When I got to the Roosevelt memorial, I took a photo of Eleanor to bring back to my group. The next time we met I passed my phone around so they could see the photos, and I played a recording of her voice. There are so many things to talk about, and so much to learn, remember, and appreciate.

The General provided this moving testimonial about our sessions, before his Alzheimer's had progressed beyond speech: "The quiet of meditation is very important. It helps me to remember what's important. Our meditation circles have taught me about many things, including love."

MEDITATION INSTRUCTION
OPENING ASPIRATION PRAYER

This aspiration prayer helps to set the intention for any group or session. It's simple, non-theistic, and universal. It also offers the opportunity to talk about what each of the words means and how people in the group experience them. This practice acknowledges and cultivates qualities that we already have and experience, and it's empowering to realize that your own kindness and love can have an effect on yourself and everyone around you.

Pause for a moment before beginning, to touch in with your posture, body, and breath. Let your mind rest on your breathing for a few breaths to help you feel more present and settled. Then, turn your mind to this Aspiration Prayer, pausing briefly between each verse to contemplate and feel its meaning.

First, feel your own presence, your breath, and how you feel, and recite:

"May love and kindness bring happiness and peace to _my_ body and mind."

Feel love and kindness toward yourself, appreciating the goodness of your body and mind.

Next, imagine someone you care about, and make this same aspiration for them:

"May love and kindness bring happiness and peace to _your_ body and mind."

Feel your love and kindness flowing out to them,

bringing happiness and ease to their body and mind.

Finally, send this same wish to everyone in the room, and extending out to everyone in the community and in the world:

"May love and kindness bring happiness and peace to the whole world."

Feel your own love and kindness radiating out, bringing peace and happiness to the whole world.

After resting in the feeling of this radiance, return your attention to your body and breath for a few moments or as long as you like.

MEDITATION INSTRUCTION
PRACTICING KINDNESS

Intentional kindness is beneficial in many ways, both to the giver and to the receiver. This practice is related to mindfulness because we are deliberately lifting ourselves out of our ruminatory, thinking grooves and using a different part of our brains, which automatically makes us, the giver of kindness, feel better. Performing acts of kindness has even been shown to help with overall health and well-being, improving resiliency, strengthening the immune system, and promoting feelings of happiness and peace. As one of my Buddhist teachers said, "If you want to be miserable, think of yourself; if you want to be happy, think of others." Experiments, and experience, support this in finding that even thinking and talking about kindness increases feelings of happiness and peace. And, as for the receiver of an act of kindness, who knows what the ripple effects will be?

So, rather than spreading aggression, impatience, irritation, and small-mindedness (which will also, always, have ripple effects), you can have the intention to notice your impulses and try to be kind instead. Everything you do has an effect, no matter your age or circumstances.

There are many simple things you can try, and here are just a few ideas for those in an assisted living context:

- ✓ Smile at someone instead of just walking by or ignoring them.
- ✓ Say hello, or good morning, or good evening.
- ✓ Listen to a friend or acquaintance, giving them your full attention and empathy.
- ✓ Notice someone who looks lonely or sad, and invite them to sit with you.
- ✓ Introduce yourself to someone you haven't met.
- ✓ Help a new resident with questions they may have.
- ✓ Be curious about other people and ask them questions about themselves.
- ✓ Hold the door or elevator for someone, if you can.
- ✓ Send a random letter, hello email, or text to a family member or friend you hardly ever see.
- ✓ Give a compliment to someone.
- ✓ Send someone a card.
- ✓ Wave to children and parents at the park.
- ✓ Say "I love you" to everyone you love.
- ✓ Do a simple favor for someone who needs help.
- ✓ Donate to good causes.

MINDFULNESS FOR SICKNESS, PAIN, AND STRESS

Sickness and pain are part of our human condition. Even though we can all expect to experience these at some point, it's always difficult to endure the discomfort, uncertainty, and fear that can naturally arise. We tend to feel immortal when we're young, and even as we age we can be caught off guard by the changes in our bodies and minds. It can feel almost insulting to develop problems like high blood pressure or cholesterol after a lifetime of relatively healthy habits, to have your hearing or eyesight diminish, to lose your hair, to notice your physical stamina and strength starting to fade, or to need your joints replaced. It's also scary, because it's all a reminder of the reality of death, which comes to us all no matter how good we may be at ignoring it.

Then there are the diseases that can seem to come out of nowhere: the cancers, various kinds of heart disease, immune system and auto-immune diseases, infections, and so many others. Falling and breaking our bones can happen in a split second and change our lives for a while or forever. And there is the very difficult issue of chronic pain, which may or may not have a clear cause and often doesn't have a clear cure.

Our western culture has had a "fix-it" mentality about sickness for a long time: take a pill or have surgery and it will go away. We get angry at doctors, ourselves, or God when cures aren't available or effective. And to make it worse, there has long been a kind of guilt associated with being sick, as if we did something wrong, somehow inflicting the disease on ourselves. I remember when cancer was a dirty word; my parents and grandparents' generations would whisper it when no one else could hear, or call it "C," or just entirely lie about it. It was somehow wrong to be sick, especially with such a fearsome disease.

Our language reflects the dichotomy between sickness and health when we talk about fighting or battling a disease, as if it's an enemy that has invaded our territory. There is a concept of winning or losing the battle rather than relating with our bodies holistically and considering a whole range of approaches in addition to medications and surgeries. Sickness and pain are part of our human condition and, while difficult, they can teach us a lot about ourselves that can benefit us in the long run. In any case, it doesn't help to be angry.

Our perspectives change when we get an illness that can't just be "fixed." I discovered this when I was 38 years old and finally crashed. I had made my way through law school with two young children, a husband who was unfaithful to our marriage, and I had just given up my job and home in Nova Scotia to help a friend in southern California who was dying of AIDS. I was emotionally and physically exhausted, and the drastic change in climate and some dehydration seem to have kicked my immune system into a collapse.

For the first few days I assumed I was just dehydrated and that the problem would be solved with plenty of liquids and some rest. But it didn't go away: dizziness, bone-deep fatigue, foggy mind, joint pain, ups and downs in body temperature. I tried to outwit it, like I had ninja mind powers, but it was strong and deep and I spiraled downward as its impact on my body grew. My sick friend finally recognized it as what was then called the Epstein-Barr virus, a precursor of what came to be known first as Chronic Fatigue Syndrome and some years later as Myalgic Encephalomyelitis (ME).

ME/CFS is a debilitating disease that doesn't get much respect, and even less so back then in late '80's and early '90's. The first doctor I saw was a patronizing, uninformed charlatan who told me I was depressed and needed Prozac. I had already studied and ruled out clinical depression and knew I was just depressed because my life was derailed, my husband found greener pastures for the final time, and I had to move back to the DC area so that my parents could help me. Over the next ten years I slowly gained back some strength and equilibrium, but I was unable to keep up my legal credentials and I worked part-time in my brother's business. That was almost 30 years ago now, and over that time I have become quite functional, only having temporary relapses once or twice a year lasting a week or two. I've had very demanding and fulfilling jobs since then that sometimes put me over the top; old habits of multi-tasking and not taking care of oneself die slowly, but I've gotten better at taking care of myself.

But the point here is that this disease changed my life because I couldn't just "fix" it or make it go away. It blew my mind; I felt terrified, sad, trapped, and confused. My sense of identity was thwarted, and the ignorant illusion of indestructibility that had fed my failure to care for my own health crumbled. I became sympathetic, for the first time, with people who regularly rested and took care of themselves. I experienced what it was like to have a disease no one could see and that most people didn't understand or appreciate.

Mindfulness is not a fix-it and should not be presented as such. But there's no question that our bodies and minds affect each other and contribute to our overall state of health. When we're in an emotional state like anger, for example, our teeth and hands may clench, our heart rate and blood pressure go up, we may sweat, and so on. Likewise, when our bodies are sick or tired, we can experience trouble concentrating and we may feel depressed or irritated, among other mental reactions.

One way to explain this is that we breathe fast when we're fearful, as if we're being chased by a tiger. In this state of fear and anxiety our brains direct our bodies to produce high levels of adrenaline and cortisol, our digestive system slows down (thus the feeling of butterflies in our stomachs), and we go into a state of high alert. Many people live in this constant state of anxiety, which takes a toll on their overall health. Deliberately slowing down our breathing tricks our amygdala into assuming we're safe, thus lowering stress hormones, heart rate, and blood pressure. When we're familiar with mindfulness, we can remember more often to catch ourselves in the middle of anxiety and breathe more slowly and deeply. Physiologically, it's been shown that slowing down our breathing and resting our attention on each in-breath and out-breath calms the parts of the brain that affect emotional states, helping to reduce anxiety and stress.

So the first benefit of mindfulness meditation is very basic: just remembering our breath gives us something familiar and neutral to rest our anxious minds on, and it has the added benefit of calming down our physical systems in a good way.

I had a cousin who was a brilliant academic with a tragedy-filled life. One of her daughters died in a car accident as a teenager, and then her abusive husband took her son away from her. When she eventually remarried and was blissfully happy, she had a stroke that almost killed her. Over time, she recovered her full brain functions and her ability to talk, but her body was partially paralyzed. Her husband took care of her and made her feel not only human but loved, hopeful, motivated, and even sexy, and in this condition she completed her PhD thesis on the effect of intellectual activity on stroke recovery. Then, one day her husband went out to get some milk and was killed in a car accident.

I flew to Denver to be with her, and we spent a lot of time lying around, sleeping and grieving, going out occasionally with her wheelchair to the hair and nail salon or just to sit in the sun. One day when I came into her bedroom, trying to coax her to drink some tea, she said that she didn't know how she could go on living. She felt that everything was too painful and hopeless and that she didn't know where to put her mind, because there was nowhere that didn't make her feel panicked and freaked out. I suggested that she just put her mind on her breathing and come back to that as much as she could or wanted to. It was a safe place for her to rest.

She told me some years later that this saved her life. She was an incredibly brave woman who lived for many more years, somehow managing to bear all of her grief and physical struggle. She influenced many people with her courage, humor, and sharp mind; she passed away a few years ago.

~

In addition to helping calm our fearful minds and relax our bodies, mindfulness also helps us tune in to how we're feeling, both physically and mentally. When we stop and observe ourselves with openness and kindness, we can be clearer about how we are and what we need. It's good to explore treatment possibilities with intelligence and an open mind, and mindfulness practice can help us work with the fear and panic that can naturally accompany health crises. Kindness and nonjudgment are key, and there are no "shoulds." We may want to try various treatment methods, or we may want to cry and hole up for a while.

There is an old Buddhist teaching about pain called the Two Arrows. The first arrow that metaphorically strikes us is the pain we naturally feel when we're sick or injured, which is actual, legitimate pain, small or large. The second arrow is the one we send to the already painful injury. This is the added layer of suffering we cause for ourselves when we react to the pain with fear, anger, shame, and other negative emotions. Another way I've seen this expressed is with this equation:

PAIN + STRUGGLE = SUFFERING

Pain is a natural part of being human and comes to all of us in some form, sooner or later. There's no getting around that. But how we struggle with it is up to us, and we can learn to identify that struggle and separate it from the pain itself. Acceptance of how we are in any given moment doesn't mean resignation, but rather a nonjudgmental openness to seeing things as they are so that we can make the best decisions about how to work with ourselves. It helps us to find the gentle strength we need to abide with the continually changing circumstances of our lives.

As always, Jon Kabat-Zinn says this beautifully in a discussion of the mindfulness practice of the body scan:

> *In the body scan, we are developing a greater intimacy with bare sensation, opening to the give-and-take embedded in the reciprocity between the sensations themselves and our awareness of them. As a result, it is not uncommon to be less disturbed by them, or disturbed by them in a different, a wiser way, even when they are acute. Awareness learns to let them be as they are and to hold them without triggering so much emotional reactivity and also so much inflamed thinking about them. We sometimes speak of awareness and discernment differentiating and perhaps naturally "uncoupling" the sensory dimension of the experience of pain from the emotional and cognitive dimensions of pain. In the process, the intensity of the sensations themselves can sometimes subside. In any event, they may come to be seen as less onerous, less debilitating.*
>
> *(from* Coming To Our Senses, *2005.)*

MEDITATION INSTRUCTION
THE PRACTICE OF LOVING ABIDING

In this practice, the word "LOVE" is used as an acronym to help remember these steps:

LOCATE - OBSERVE - VALIDATE - EMBRACE

Begin by settling yourself comfortably (sitting or lying down), and rest for a few moments as you bring your attention to your own natural breathing. Then, follow these steps, as slowly or briefly as you like:

1. LOCATE: Find a sensation in your body that you want to focus on for this practice. This may take a little time as you begin to slow down and tune in to the different parts of yourself. Choose one.

2. OBSERVE: Then, observe it without attaching names or judgments to it. Just notice where it is in your body, how small or large an area it takes up, what its temperature feels like, how strong it is, whether it feels sharp, dull, pulsating, intermittent or constant, and so on. This kind of observation has the mindful qualities of being curious, interested, and caring, as well as nonjudgmental.

3. VALIDATE: Accept this feeling, as it is. Accept that you are experiencing it, as only you can. It is happening; you feel it. No one else can tell you how to experience it; there are no "shoulds."

4. EMBRACE: Rest with this feeling, just as you are experiencing

it, directly and personally. Notice if you start thinking about it, talking to yourself, rather than just being with it. As you breathe in, imagine you are breathing into the feeling, embracing it and accepting it; and as you breathe out, rest in your awareness of the feeling and relax into the space around you. You are breathing healing oxygen into the sensation, and breathing out tension, fear, and thoughts about the sensation. You are embracing it as you would an injured child you are holding and comforting. Continue with this for as long as you like. When your mind wanders, just come back to it gently.

Then, let go of this practice and just rest in an overall awareness of your body and breath, for as long as you like. When you're ready, get up gently and go forward into your day.

MEDITATION INSTRUCTION

VISUALIZATIONS: The River, The Lake, and The Mountain

Visualization within the context of basic mindfulness meditation is an experiential way to tap into basic positive qualities and strengthen them within oneself. Imagery can also be an especially helpful and soothing anchor for the mind when it is restless and disturbed. It's important to do any visualization practice within the context of mindfulness meditation, so that the mind is stable enough to be able to focus on the imagery.

The following three visualizations embody the three principle aspects, or outcomes, of mindfulness meditation: stability (The River), clarity (The Lake), and strength (The Mountain). Becoming familiar with these visualizations can create lasting images and feelings that remind us of these inherent aspects of ourselves as we navigate the ups and downs of our lives. I have written each one here in a complete form that can be read just as it is, though each person's visualization will be unique. You'll notice that the beginning is always the same: settling yourself and briefly resting your mind on your breathing. Take your time and enjoy.

THE RIVER (STABILITY)

Find a quiet place where you can be undisturbed for a little while. Close the door, turn off your phone, and give yourself a set amount of time—fifteen or twenty minutes—for this restful contemplation.

Take your time. Pause as much as you like to rest in the descriptions of where you are, what you are doing, the images, sounds, and smells.

Gently close your eyes and imagine yourself in a small boat on a busy river that's full of rocks and rushing water. The loud sound of the water fills your ears, and you strain to hear the clamoring of people in other boats calling out to you and to each other. Your attention is constantly being pulled between the demands of navigating your own boat around the dangerous rocks and eddies and the shiftiness of other boats coming in and out of your field of awareness. Feel the tension in your body and mind as you imagine being in this situation, your muscles straining to keep your boat from colliding or capsizing, your eyes stinging with the spraying water as you struggle with all of this chaos just to keep going. Even when you come to a span of relatively calm water, you know that you have to be on the alert for potential dangers lurking. The river is constantly moving and changing.

Contemplate this for a few minutes. It's the busyness, shiftiness, uncertainty, and clamor of your daily life. It's your everyday struggle, and you can feel it in your body and mind.

Now, for some reason, you have the idea that you could pull your boat over to the river bank. You hardly noticed the banks before, because you were so preoccupied with staying safely afloat in the river and didn't really consider an alternative. This thought comes as a revelation to you, and you pull your boat gently to the side and secure it there. You feel lonely and a little unsure about doing this because everyone else is going ahead with their usual river activity. You wonder if stopping like this will make you fall behind in your endeavors and if the others will outpace you in some way. But you feel a curiosity, a wonder, and also some unnameable trust that this is something you should not ignore. So you climb out of your boat and step onto the earth.

As you climb up the gently sloping, grassy bank, the noisy sounds of the river begin to fade; and as you sit down in the warm sun, you are dazzled by the quiet and the stillness. For a few minutes you feel a little dizzy, adjusting to this contrast from constant movement, noise, and preoccupation with your survival on the water. You take a few deep breaths, feel the earth beneath you, the warm sun on your face, and a sense of safety as you rest in the refreshing stillness. The sense of spinning gradually subsides, and you relax completely, where you are.

Within that silence and stillness, you begin to become aware of things you haven't been able to notice before: the leaves and grasses making different sounds as they're moved by the breeze; the birds calling from near and far in infinite layers of sound; the vastness of the sky above you; the scents of the wildflowers and the fragrance of the fertile earth; the feeling of your body as it shifts in the simple pleasures of being alive; and the subtle, intimate beating of your own heart. You feel a sense of wakefulness and tenderness in this ordinary, yet vivid, experience.

Turning your awareness to the feeling of your breathing, continue to rest there by the river for a minute or two, or as long as you like, as you gently breathe in and out. When your mind habitually wanders back to your struggles on the river, acknowledge that with kindness and return very simply to where you are—sitting and breathing on your peaceful river bank.

Finally, gently open your eyes, stretch your body, and rejoin your daily activities with the knowledge that the river is just part of a great landscape. Rather than being a burden, you can enjoy it as a challenge and a delight. The peaceful riverbank is always with you.

This perspective can help to open your eyes to the greater reality in which you live, but which you may often forget in your struggle to navigate your life. In every moment, you can pause to rest on the peaceful riverbank and remember to breathe, look up and see the sky, feel the breezes and strong winds, and feel the beat of your own heart. The more you become accustomed to this way of being, the more you will naturally carry it into every moment of your life.

THE LAKE (CLARITY)

Find a quiet place where you can be undisturbed for a little while. Close the door, turn off your phone, and give yourself a set amount of time—fifteen or twenty minutes—for this restful contemplation. Settle your body, check your posture, and rest your mind on your natural breathing for a minute or two.

Now turn to the contemplation of The Lake. Relax and take your time. Pause whenever you like to rest in the descriptions of where you are, what you are doing, the images, sounds, and smells.

Gently close your eyes and imagine yourself in a small boat in the middle of a large lake. It's a cloudy, stormy day, and what you thought would be an enjoyable break from your usual stress has turned into the same old tiring struggle. It's a little too cold, the water is choppy, and all you can hear is the wind whipping around your ears and the waves slapping against your boat, which is bumping up and down and rocking from side to side. The water is so stirred up that you can't see into it; it just looks agitated, murky and gray. Your clothes are getting damp and you feel cold, anxious, and irritated. No one else is out on the lake or on the shores, as far as you can tell, and you feel alone, tired, and a little worried.

Contemplate this for a minute or two. This represents the familiar struggle of your daily life, the times when you don't feel relaxed or at ease because so many things are coming at you. It can even make you feel a little seasick at times. You can't really see or hear anything around you because you are spending all of your energy on the immediate difficult situation, compounded by stress and the emotions that are being triggered.

Now imagine that the weather is starting to change. The wind is starting to die down, the air feels warmer, and the storm clouds move away and begin to disperse. The patches of blue sky grow larger and the sun finally breaks through and lights everything up. The air becomes warm and calm, and your little boat stops rocking and rests quietly on the surface of the lake. Welcoming this change, you relax in your boat and start to look around you.

The sky is a brilliant blue, and the warm sun shines down on your face and body. You close your eyes for a moment and feel the nourishing heat penetrating all the way into your bones and organs. You take a deep breath, feeling that you can relax at last.

The water is calm and your boat is still. You look out to the shores of the lake, where there are now people and families, playing and resting. Their distant shouts and laughter drift out to you, softly, and you watch them for a little while, interested in their activities. A little farther away you see some cows grazing in a pasture, and you can hear an occasional cowbell as they gently move from place to place. Farther off you notice the faint sound of a mower, not loud enough to disturb the tranquility of the lake.

Then you bring your attention back to where you are, in your peaceful little boat. You breathe in the fragrant smell of the lake and the gentle breeze and again feel the pleasant warmth of the sun on your skin. You notice that the surface of the lake is now completely still and smooth, and that its previously stirred-up water has settled and become clear. As you look down into the lake, you are surprised and delighted to realize that you can see everything, as the sun shines through the clear water and illuminates the sandy bottom, the beautiful, gently waving underwater plants, the occasional fish swimming by, and even a few bits of trash and a bottle or two.

Like your mind when it is settled, in the clarity of the still and illumined lake you can see everything. With unbiased mindfulness you are simply curious; without needing to label things as good or bad, you appreciate simply being able to *see*.

As you rest there, turn your awareness to the feeling of your breathing. When your mind habitually wanders back to your struggles in the storm, acknowledge that with kindness and return very simply to where you are, breathing and resting in your comfortable little boat on the calm, clear lake.

Finally, when you're ready, you can imagine your boat drifting gently into the shore, where you step onto the beach, stretch, and look around you. As you rejoin your daily activities, you can carry the peaceful clarity and luminosity of the lake with you, as the clear and settled nature of your own mind. It's always available to you.

THE MOUNTAIN (STRENGTH)

Find a quiet place where you can be undisturbed for a little while.

Close the door, turn off your phone, and give yourself a set amount of time—fifteen or twenty minutes—for this restful contemplation. Settle your body, check your posture, and rest your mind on your natural breathing for a minute or two.

Now turn to the contemplation of The Mountain. Relax and take your time. Pause whenever you like to rest in the descriptions of where you are, what you are doing, the images, sounds, and smells.

Close your eyes and feel your wholeness and strength as you sit and breathe. Pause and rest with your body and breath for as long as you like.

Now imagine, in your mind's eye, a beautiful mountain, either one you have seen or an imaginary one. Take a little time to make it vivid in your mind, noticing the details of its slopes, its peaks, the sky around it, and the earth from which it rises. Your mountain may have high, snow-covered peaks, or it could be a gentle, forest-covered mountain. Whatever it is, let yourself rest with the image of your beautiful mountain. Sometimes you may experience it as very close, and sometimes farther away. Relax in the presence of your mountain.

As you sit here, feel the strength and stillness of your mountain. It is immovable and unwavering, no matter what happens around it. Now let yourself move toward the mountain and merge with it, so that you actually become the mountain: your head is the peak, up in the sky; your shoulders and arms are its slopes; your torso is its main body; and your seat and legs are its strong and stable base, interconnected with the vast earth all around and beneath it. Feel yourself as the mountain, still and peaceful as you rest in this natural state.

And now, as the mountain, you can notice how the clouds are moving around you, sometimes bringing rain or snow as they alternate with the clear blue sky. When it's morning, the dawn brings the light and warmth of the sun to your peaks and slopes, and the sun moves and intensifies as the day advances, strongest and brightest in the early afternoon. As evening approaches, the shadows begin to lengthen, the air cools, and, as the sky grows darker, the moon and stars appear in the canopy above you.

You can imagine how the seasons come and go, as you remain ever still and present: the cold and snow of winter; the new growth and fertility of spring; the heat and activity of summer; the abundance and poignancy of autumn. Sometimes the sky is clear and bright, and sometimes you feel completely shrouded in mist. Sometimes the air is still, and at other times there are fierce winds and blinding storms. Through all of this, you remain as the mountain, calm and still.

All sorts of things can happen on your mountain: wildlife of all kinds are born, live, and die; flowers and trees bloom and change through the seasons; people can come and picnic on you, sometimes leaving trash behind, sometimes being respectful and caring. You are still the mountain, dignified and beautiful, as you are.

The strength and stillness of the mountain abide in you, and by spending time with this visualization you can more easily access and embody all of these natural qualities. So just rest with this image and feeling of yourself as the mountain, for as long as you like. It is who you are.

Finally, let the image and feeling of the mountain dissolve into your heart and abide there. Returning your awareness to your actual human body, feel your body breathing, feel your whole body sitting on the earth, and rest there in the stillness with your attention on your breathing for a few minutes. As you gradually open your eyes, and then begin to rejoin your daily activities, you can carry with you the feeling of the strength and inner stillness of the mountain. This peaceful strength is always available to you.

(I have adapted this from a longer version by Jon Kabat-Zinn, which you can easily find on the internet. He also has a free 20-minute audio version at soundcloud.com/devicer23/01-jon-kabat-zinn-mountain, among other sites.)

CULTIVATING COMPASSION

In our new, connected world, we're constantly being reminded of the intense suffering and unease that's happening everywhere, every day. Some of it is hard to imagine and some of it hits all too close to home. It comes in the context of wars, natural disasters, climate change, politics, relationships, workplace, family, sickness, accidents, shootings, and countless other things. In today's environment, it can be too easy to feel frustrated, even hopeless at times, about what we can do to help. How can we feel so much suffering without becoming either numb or debilitated? And how can we be compassionate in a way that provides relief and effects change?

"Compassion" is a word that's loosely used to mean anything from caring about the suffering of others, to stepping out to help those in need, to simply smiling and being nice.* All of the major world religions and traditions consider compassion to be one of the greatest and most important qualities a human being must have in order to live a meaningful and virtuous life. It's an energy that links us together as human beings because of our mutual experience of sickness, change, anxiety, grief, and the countless other ways in which we suffer.

At its heart, though, compassion is more than an attitude or a philosophy; it's a practice, an activity, the "walk" of our talk. It's a deep sympathy that can't help but manifest in our words and actions when we are brave enough to feel and acknowledge the pain of human existence. It's a way of being, an atmosphere that marks someone as a "compassionate person."

The word "compassion" derives from the Latin words *com/cum*, meaning "with," and *passus/pati*, referring to "suffering." Thus, compassion means "to suffer together with another." (The English noun "patient" comes from the same root and literally means "one who suffers." The word *passion* also originally meant suffering, often associated with some kind of intense volitional force as in the "Passion of Christ," etc. Not until the 16th century does it appear to have shifted to its more modern meaning of intense desire, though still connected with that notion of an almost uncontrollable force.)

So we must actually feel and understand the suffering of another to be fully engaged in true compassion. That's why, in the Buddhist tradition, compassion is considered to be inseparable from emptiness, which means that it goes beyond mere ideas of what we *should* feel or do or what we merely *think* another person needs. (*Emptiness* in Buddhism generally refers to being empty of conceptual content, which by its nature is limited.) Authentic compassion is based on experience and awakened intelligence, the entire mind/heart of our being, which naturally manifests in our thoughts, words, and actions. As the well-known Vietnamese Buddhist teacher Thich Nhat Hanh has said, "Compassion is a verb."

Spiritual traditions have long held compassion to be central to union with godliness and, on a more relative level, to leading a principled life. In the Muslim tradition, God (Allah) is referred to as Al-Rahim, which means "The Compassionate," and almost all of the 114 chapters of the Quran begin with the verse, "In the name of Allah the Compassionate, the Merciful." These virtues of compassion and mercy are considered inseparable from God-ness.

Similarly, in Judaism, God is described in Exodus as "compassionate and gracious, slow to anger and abundant in kindness and truth, preserver of kindness for thousands of generations..."

This verse is taught extensively in synagogues as the detailed "13 Attributes of Compassion." The closest earthly correlation to this kind of fundamental compassion is said to be the feeling of parents for their children.

In the Christian religion, God is referred to as the "Father of compassion" and the "God of all comfort" (2nd Corinthians). The verse goes on to say that God "comforts us in all our troubles, so that we can comfort those in any trouble with the comfort we ourselves received from God." Jesus embodies true compassion in consistently disregarding his own comfort in order to relieve the suffering of others, including various kinds of societal outcasts. One of the essential teachings of Christianity is the "golden rule," which exhorts us to imagine how we would feel before committing an act that affects someone else. ("Do unto others as you would have them do unto you.") Versions of this teaching show up in some form in all wisdom traditions, pointing up how basic it is to our universal human experience. Being able to imagine how other human beings feel is central to a decent and cohesive human society, which includes meaningful communication and creative, compassion-based activity.

In Buddhism, too, compassion is considered to be basic to our humanness, existing even before our conditioned thoughts and emotions. It is the way we naturally are when our minds/hearts are unobstructed by confused thoughts and emotions related to our own self-preservation. Without this ability to feel the suffering of others as connected to ourselves, the basic, innate sanity of our humanness is not fully realized. Since everyone suffers in some way because of the impermanent, changing nature of everything (including ourselves), mindfulness of our own fears and anxieties can foster more awareness of similar struggles in other people. This naturally opens our perspective to one of increased empathy and compassion.

~

While kindness and compassion are most often associated with gentle behavior that promotes harmony and healing, compassionate activity can sometimes include saying "No." For example, when a child reaches for a hot stove, you instinctively jump to prevent her from hurting herself without trying to pad that No in niceties. You just slice through the harmful action as abruptly and effectively as you can. This No is what distinguishes true compassion from simply being "nice," which can sometimes cause us to enable harmful behaviors. Fear of the No perpetuates abusive relationships, for example, because we can too easily confuse love and kindness with allowing someone to harm us, which ultimately reinforces and harms the abuser as well. Our kindness can become a habit, almost like an addiction that feeds someone else's (and our own) dependent, familiar behaviors. It's like that saying about the devil you know being more comfortable than an unknown alternative–it can feel like jumping off a cliff to step out of one's familiar cocoon, no matter how hellish that cocoon is.

Saying No in these situations isn't aggressive or unkind, although it may be taken in that way by someone accustomed to being enabled. We tell our children No because we love them. We set boundaries that provide the possibility for protection and a healthy, safe environment. This can be the grandest, most courageous act of compassion when a situation calls for it, and it can also be very ordinary and obvious.

Whether we're dealing with a small, everyday boundary (like, "No, I really don't need another ice cream sundae," or "No, I can't stay in bed and miss work again," etc.) or a larger one that threatens serious harm, we can approach our own compassionate No with kindness and strength. In the Buddhist teachings, this form of compassion is said to transcend the traditional precepts–like not lying, stealing, etc.– when doing so is necessary to reduce the harm. For example, it may be appropriate to break the precept of not stealing if you are taking away an alcoholic's stash of liquor. It can be necessary to lie if you are leaving an abusive partner in the safest way you can. These are not acts of cruelty; they are quite the opposite in their brilliant courage that cuts the harmful cycle of addictive co-dependency. This kind of compassion is difficult and even outrageous, and it can leave you feeling groundless and shaky. It is a last resort when it becomes clear that nothing else will work, or that harm is imminent. Sometimes that clarity happens very quickly, and sometimes it may take a while.

*A word about "smiling and being nice": There's a lot to be said for this, too, and it can definitely be the most compassionate thing one can do at times. On the other hand, it can be a fearful way of avoiding confrontation, so this is actually an important dynamic to notice more in ourselves. Ancient conventional wisdom about this is articulated in many contexts, including the Hippocratic Oath from the medical tradition: "First, do no harm." The Buddhist teachings express it like this, in a nutshell: You may not be able to help someone, but at least try not to make things worse. As the Dalai Lama says, "If you can, help others; if you cannot do that, at least do not harm them."

Mindfulness-awareness meditation helps us to see how we perpetuate confusion in our own minds, and we begin by becoming more familiar with those patterns and aspiring not to create more pollution, or harm, in the world. We begin to see our automatic responses before we act on them, which is a seismic change in awareness. "Clear seeing," known in Sanskrit as *vipashyana*, is the outcome of mindfulness-awareness meditation, the intelligence of realizing that our thoughts are not solid. In this way, we have the opportunity to see what is actually going on, and what someone really needs, beyond our preconceived ideas. This greater awareness is what allows true compassion to arise.

~

One of the special things about Buddhism is that it gives us tools for actively cultivating positive qualities, including compassion. This is based on the view that compassion is an inherent aspect of human nature and it can therefore be actively cultivated. By evoking our own experience of compassion, however small, we can work to consciously strengthen and expand it. The ultimate view in Buddhism is to feel equal compassion for all beings. So we start with what we have, where we are. We can all feel suffering in some way, and by realizing that even one other person, or animal, suffers, and having the true wish that they be free from that suffering, we are cultivating compassion.

As I mentioned above, one of the benefits of mindfulness-awareness meditation is that it helps us to see our habitual mental patterns. This is profound because, for the first time, we begin to see how we are not our thoughts, and we don't have to be propelled and controlled by them. In addition to meditation, there are many practices that can help us see the gross and subtle ways in which we cause harm. For example, we can practice not lying or otherwise causing hurt with our speech; not killing or harming living beings; not enabling others in ways that perpetuate harmful behaviors; not craving more than we really need; and deliberately cultivating other ways to raise our awareness of our own habitual behaviors. This isn't a moralistic thing to do, where we judge ourselves as good or bad, but is a skillful way of setting boundaries for ourselves so that we can become more aware of our mindless habits.

Alternatively, a simple way we can practice raising our awareness of positive actions is to make a practice of performing ordinary acts of kindness, like smiling at someone, holding a door or letting someone go before us, taking time to thank someone verbally or in writing, and so many other, endless ways we can strengthen our ability to act intentionally, or consciously. Each time we do this, we send out ripples of kindness instead of chain reactions of confusion. But in order to do even these things, we have to have an ability to notice our habitual, mindless behaviors, and deliberately shift them. So mindfulness is the basis.

In addition to working directly upon our experiential awareness, neuroscientists are discovering that increasing compassion through contemplative practices changes the brain and leads to increased empathy and contentment, more harmonious relationships, and a decrease in depression–all of which have implications for bullying and other forms of aggressive behaviors. Compassion not only helps the objects of our compassion, but it makes us happier as well. And this kind of happiness, or contentment, has great implications for our physical and mental health, like lower blood pressure, better sleep, more productivity, better emotional regulation, and many other benefits.

~

As the Dalai Lama says, "If you want others to be happy, practice compassion. If you want to be happy, practice compassion." Practicing hatred is a lose-lose endeavor. When we aspire to open our hearts and act with kindness and compassion, the whole world wins. It is something we can actually do in these troubled times.

MEDITATION INSTRUCTION
THE PRACTICE OF LOVING-KINDNESS AND COMPASSION

Sit in a quiet place and let your attention rest on your breathing for a minute or so. Just relax and follow each breath as it comes in and goes out. When thoughts arise, let them go and return to your breathing.

When you have settled a little, bring to mind a situation where you experienced the suffering of someone you care for. This can be a person or an animal, but let it be a real situation, past or present. Their suffering can be physical or psychological, and since this is someone you care for you can actually feel it, and it causes you to suffer, too. Evoke that feeling now, visualizing that being in your mind's eye, and send out the wish that they could be happy and free from suffering. As you send this loving and compassionate wish to them, imagine that you can see them relaxing, enjoying happiness and relief from suffering.

As you imagine this, holding the image of the person or being you have chosen in your mind, repeat to yourself again and again the following phrase:

"May [so-and-so] be happy and free from suffering."

When you notice that your mind has wandered, return to the mental image of your loved one and continue reciting this phrase. Think of how that being suffers and fervently wish them to be free from suffering and all of the causes of suffering, and imagine them being relaxed and at ease.

When you have connected with this feeling of love and compassion, think of someone you feel indifferent toward and try to generate those same feelings for them. Imagine them standing next to your loved one, in front of you, and repeat the same wish for them:

"May [this person] be happy and free from suffering."

Then, imagine someone who has harmed you in some way, who irritates you or has caused you some kind of hurt. This is a difficult contemplation, so don't start off with the most painful situation you can think of. Imagine this person with the first two, all of them looking at you with gratitude and openness, and think to yourself:

"May [so-and-so] be happy and free from suffering."

Contemplate each of these three scenarios for a few minutes. Then, imagining all three of the people standing together, relaxed and open, imagine yourself joining them, and send yourself the same wish to be happy and free from suffering:

"May I be happy and free from suffering."

Finally, expand that wish to all beings, near and far, wishing that they all experience happiness and freedom from suffering. Whoever they are, they are beings much like yourself, with hopes and fears, pain and pleasure. Include yourself in the circle of appreciation and kindness, wishing relief and freedom from suffering for yourself as well. Finally, radiate that wish out to everyone, as far as you can, thinking:

"May all beings enjoy happiness and freedom from suffering."

Feel the love and compassion radiate in all directions, for a little while.

Finally, just let it go and rest simply with your breathing.

MEDITATION INSTRUCTION
SUN (MOON) MEDITATION

1. SUN MEDITATION

✓ You can do this practice anywhere, sitting or lying down.
✓ Begin by settling yourself with quiet awareness of your breathing.

✓ Then imagine yourself in a peaceful, natural setting, where you can be undisturbed. It's a warm, fresh day, and as you rest quietly you can feel the sun on your skin. As you rest there longer, the sun's healing warmth soaks through your clothes and begins to warm your whole body, not only outside but inside. Invite it into your body, into your organs and bones, bringing you peace and comfort.

✓ If you have any area of particular pain or discomfort, you can focus on that for a while, feeling the warmth begin to relax and ease your pain. Do this for as long as you like.

✓ Then, think of someone you care about and imagine them near you, soaking in the warm, healing rays of the sun, feeling the ease and comfort the warmth brings to their mind and body. They can carry this warmth in their heart center wherever they go.

✓ Next, extend the rays out to everyone in the room or building with you, and gradually out to the whole world. Feel the sense of warmth and relaxation this brings to the whole environment.

✓ Finally, imagine the sun's healing rays dissolving into your heart center, and remaining there as a warm glow. This is always available to you.

2. SUN MEDITATION (INSTANTANEOUS)

Whenever you like, and especially if you're feeling depressed or sad, simply remember the sun in your heart and feel its warmth and light radiate through your body. Lengthen your spine, take a good breath, look around, and let the sun gently outshine the darkness. This just takes a few seconds, and can be called "remembering the sun in your heart."

3. MOON MEDITATION

If you have a physical or mental condition that feels too hot, or you want to do this practice for someone else who would benefit from cooling, you can replace the sun with the moon. Rather than being warm and golden like the sun, the moon's silvery rays are cool, healing, and soothing. Do the practice in the same way, imagining yourself outside on a pleasant, clear, and peaceful night, bathing in the moonlight.

MINDFULNESS IN EVERYDAY LIFE

The main point of practicing mindfulness-awareness meditation is to benefit yourself and your world. That may seem like a lofty goal, but if you limit your meditation practice to the occasional mental escape, like a mini-vacation or visit to the spa, its effect is only temporary and its usefulness unclear. The return to your stressful responsibilities can almost immediately overwhelm any sense of benefit from the meditation session.

What does it mean, then, to "benefit yourself and your world" by meditating regularly? Escape-type meditations, like gentle guided visualizations and sounds, can help people to relax, escape from the loop of stressful thoughts, and calm their breathing and heart rate. This is all helpful and at times is what's most needed. But mindfulness-awareness meditation fosters a deeper, more systemic change that benefits our bodies and our minds and ultimately helps others.

This systemic change comes from realizing that there is nowhere better than this present moment. You might imagine or wish for something else, but there's no getting around the fact that you are only alive right now. If you're chronically unaware of this truth, you dwell in a mental picture, or idea, of yourself and your life, instead of engaging bravely and openly with what's actually happening. You practice letting go of this made-up story by engaging in mindfulness meditation. Every time you notice your habitual thoughts and bring your attention back to here, now–your body, your breath, your senses–you're taking the reins of your life and riding its energy with awareness.

Therefore, it's important to understand what you are doing when you sit down to meditate. Rather than trying to escape your life, or yourself, you are stopping to meet yourself in a simple and direct way, just as you are. You may feel good, or anxious, or angry–many things–but you embody kindness to yourself just in the simple act of sitting down and letting yourself be, as you are, in that moment. It's a simple act and yet it's revolutionary and transformative. Whatever thoughts and feelings come up during the session, they are greeted kindly, neither pushed away nor followed. Then you return to your breath and body, again and again, just here, right now.

Every time you notice that you were caught in thoughts, carried away from this simple present situation of sitting and breathing, you strengthen your ability to be wakeful during your life. If you live your life without any awareness of what you are thinking, you are almost like a robot, driven from one thought to the next in an endless and mindless chain reaction. Waking up to your thoughts as thoughts empowers you to have choices in your responses, rather than only habitual, conditioned reactions.

The well-known holocaust survivor and neurologist Viktor Frankl, author of *Man's Search for Meaning*, said: "Between stimulus and response, there is a space. In that space is our power to choose our response. In our response lies our growth and our freedom."

This takes strength, because the energies of our lives are strong and often unsettling. The more we practice being in the brilliant space that lies outside of our familiar nest of thoughts, the more thoroughly and effectively we can engage with our lives.

Paying attention to where we are and what we're doing also relates to the issue of multi-tasking, which many of us do not only at work but in our lives. Because our brains can only process one thing at a time, micro-second by micro-second, we're actually fracturing our attention when we "multi-task" and reducing our overall effectiveness. Changing our habits and being more present for each thing we're doing, or each person we're talking to, is satisfying, calming, and yes, efficient. We can use every event and every moment of our lives to practice the wakefulness that mindfulness brings.

~

Here's one final story about joining mindfulness with a life event. When I was working at the studio in Bethesda, someone contacted us about doing a session for a bridal party on the morning of the wedding. The studio owner asked me to figure this out, and in my Google research I noticed that it has become a thing to have a calming yoga session before a wedding. I didn't find anything about meditation sessions, but I knew that I wanted to help the bride and make her feel special. The only information I had about this group ahead of time was that it included the bride, her mother, and six bridesmaids, and that they wanted it to have a theme called "Love begins at home."

The studio owner sold them a package which included a 45-minute session followed by a small champagne reception. It turned out that they didn't drink because they were strict Christians, and I found out later that the wedding was held at the Trump Hotel downtown.

This seemed to be the bride's idea, and some of them–especially the mother–were skeptical when they arrived. In fact, it seemed like the bride's mother had come against her better judgment, because at first she wouldn't smile or make eye contact with me. They had said that they wanted to sit on cushions on the floor, which I arranged in a circle with a flower arrangement and some colored markers in the middle. I gave them a brief overview of what we'd be doing, then asked them to go around and share their names, what their roles were in the wedding, what their relationship was to the bride and how long they had known her, and how they were feeling on this wedding morning.

Mostly they said they were happy, nervous, excited, and tired. They were glad to take this quiet time to be with each other and ground themselves before the day's intense activities.

I said a few things about mindfulness, remembering to breathe and relax, and we had a spacious period with a simple body scan and some guided meditation. I encouraged them to notice their thoughts and worries, and just let their minds rest on their own breathing, which they could do any time during the day: just stop and breathe, and enjoy.

Since they had this theme of "Love begins at home," I had printed an 8-1/2 x 11 poster board with that slogan on top in a nice design, and the bride's name and wedding date at the bottom. Then we did a contemplation that would fill in the middle of the poster. I gave them each a pre-cut paper petal, and the bride received the round center of the flower. I asked them to contemplate the qualities of the bride that would bring goodness and longevity to her marriage, to think of an image that represented this, and then to draw that image on their petal. The bride was instructed to draw something in the center of the flower that represented her hopes and dreams for her marriage, a sort of reminder that she could refer to during the ups and downs of life. So they spent a few minutes contemplating the bride, and when they were ready, they chose colors to draw their images. This was all done silently. When they were finished, I asked them to write a word or short phrase on their petal as well which encapsulated the feeling or meaning of their image. We then had a final round where each of them described their image and word, and the environment was filled with love and appreciation for the bride and all of her wonderful qualities. There was both laughter and tears, and everyone–especially the bride's mother–was touched. We had really honored the bride and tuned into her strengths, and to the appreciation and love everyone there had for her.

As they gathered outside in the lounge for their reception, I glued the parts of the flower onto the page and put it in a frame to present to the bride as a keepsake. They had such a good time that they stayed for almost an hour, talking about what they had done and many other things. I'm still amazed that they somehow chose to do this, and I was delighted it turned out so well for them. It was a peaceful, meaningful, and celebratory way to spend an hour on such an important and intense day.

~

One of my weekly meditation groups is for people who belong to the hospital's seniors association. Throughout our hour-long sessions we often hear ambulance sirens as people are brought in to the emergency room. Instead of regarding the noise as a disturbance, we use it as a reminder of the suffering in the world, and we send our compassion to whoever is being brought in at that moment. In mindfulness, we're not trying to escape from the events of our lives–the sounds, sights, relationships, emotions, activities. Ultimately, when our awareness is stable and strong, we can be fully and thoroughly present for every moment of our precious lives.

MEDITATION INSTRUCTION
WALKING MEDITATION

Mindfulness-awareness meditation creates the simplest situation possible: you are sitting still, preferably in a relatively undisturbed place, with your body, breath, and mind. In this way, you have an opportunity to see how your thoughts come and go, and how your attention shifts from "away" to "here," back and forth, again and again. That is the practice, the awareness of your mind and body through your many moods. Over time you become more stable in your ability to be presently aware and engaged with where you are and what you're doing.

As soon as you get up from your meditation seat, however,

your mind can already be out of the door, checking your messages, on to the next thing. Awareness while sitting still is one thing; maintaining that while we're moving and interacting is quite another.

Walking meditation provides a powerful bridge between sitting still and entering fully into your life. While still in the protected space of meditation, you can add the activity of walking and practice being attentive to that. Rather than having breath as your focus, or reference point, you use the feeling of walking. Specifically, you notice your feet touching the floor, one after the other, and the feeling of your legs and body moving through the space as you walk. As in sitting meditation, you will notice occasionally or frequently, that your mind has wandered from what you are actually doing. At that point, you very simply return to your walking meditation.

Walking meditation is also used in longer meditation sessions to provide a physical break, an opportunity to move the body. I started including it in the 45-minute sessions in the mindfulness studios, because those longer sessions were a little onerous for new people. It's still a practice of awareness and includes good posture: upright and relaxed. Your eyes are open with a lowered gaze, so that you're not occupying yourself with visual entertainment. In that way, you have an awareness of the room and your walking meditation companions, and at the same time you are maintaining mindfulness of your steps, your posture, and your thoughts.

Walking meditation is done at a medium pace. Hands are held at the level of the waist, with one hand cupping the other. This is both comfortable and simple. The transition from sitting to walking, and back to sitting, is done in silence, because it's all part of the formal meditation period. You can also practice walking meditation on your own.

MEDITATION INSTRUCTION
FINDING TIME TO MEDITATE

Meditation can be done on your own or with a group, in settings ranging from your home to your office, a studio or meditation center in the city, or a retreat setting in the countryside. Here are a few helpful hints you can try for supporting your intention to practice meditation:

Place: At home, try to have a quiet, uncluttered place you can go without having to constantly rearrange things. Removing obstacles to practice is key, so keep it simple. At work, it's important that you feel comfortable and safe, not edgy about someone walking in. Do your best to find a place where you can have some consistency.

Time: Try a time that might work within your schedule, and if it doesn't seem to work try other times. Everyone is different, so don't give up and don't be too rigid. Put your meditation sessions on your calendar and reserve the time as best as you can. Notice whether your excuses are real or just a form of resistance–no judgment!

Length: It's better to schedule short sessions so that you're more likely to do them and enjoy them. Then, if you have more time on a weekend, for example, you can schedule a longer session. Again, everyone is different and the point here is to be realistic: neither too lazy nor too ambitious or demanding of yourself. Gentle persistence, discipline with a sense of humor, intention with a light touch, are good reminders.

Format: Think about what you want to do. Some people like to use a meditation App for guidance, others want to sit and breathe, and others may connect with or want to try other mindfulness practices. It's important to be thoughtful and clear about what you're doing in any given session.

Retreats: Unless a retreat is specifically advertised for beginners, it's important to have a good relationship with your meditation practice before putting yourself into something more intense. Group retreats can be a wonderful way to deepen your connection with your practice, so do your research about the teachers, schedule, environment, and so on. Talk to an experienced meditation instructor for advice. You may also like to do a private mini-retreat, where you block off a day or half-day to meditate, walk, read, do a little yoga, and be silent.

Within you, there is a stillness and a sanctuary to which you can retreat at any time and be yourself.
                                        - Hermann Hesse (1877-1962)

QUESTIONS AND ANSWERS

◦ WHAT IS MINDFULNESS?

Mindfulness is the inherent capacity of the human mind to be completely present, focused, and engaged in any moment of life. It's the bright awareness that is interested, alert, open, nonjudgmental, and caring. We're not mindful much of the time because of the way our minds instantaneously and habitually filter and evaluate everything we perceive, based on our conditioning and past experiences. Instead of experiencing the world around us, we engage in a persistent, subconscious process of reshaping it to fit our preconceptions and make it familiar. When we are unaware of this, it's as if we're seeing and experiencing our lives through dark glasses, with a t.v. blaring inside of our heads. Being intentionally present helps quiet the t.v. and remove the dark glasses, bringing us a sense of calm and clarity.

◦ WHAT IS MINDFULNESS MEDITATION?

In mindfulness meditation, you deliberately focus your attention on a chosen object, such as the breath, and then notice when your mind has wandered from that focus. There is no other goal in mindfulness practice than to come back, again and again, to the object of meditation.

167

Thoughts are not regarded as problematic or as interfering with the practice but are a natural part of the experience. Noticing that we're caught in them, however, rather than being present and aware of where we actually are, is what distinguishes mindfulness from other practices. Mindfulness meditation calms and strengthens the mind, and over time you become more and more familiar with the way your mind works. And as your habits start to shift, it's more natural to be present than it is to be mentally absent.

' HOW IS MINDFULNESS MEDITATION DIFFERENT FROM TM AND OTHER KINDS OF MEDITATION?

TM (Transcendental Meditation) uses a mantra (sound/word) as the object of meditation, and when the mind wanders the attention is brought back to this mantra. So it's similar to mindfulness meditation in that regard, sharing the physiological and experiential benefits of calming the mind and body, etc. The overall view is a little different, however, because TM has the goal of "automatic self-transcending," or experiencing the true self. Even though that is basically what's happening in pure mindfulness meditation, the only real goal is to continually come back to the present moment and rest in that, relinquishing the habitual tendency to dwell in thoughts and fantasies.

' WHY DO WE USE THE BREATH AS OUR OBJECT OF MEDITATION?

An object of meditation can be a physical object, like a candle, stone, or statue. It can also be a word (like a mantra), an image (visualization), or a particular thought. The breath, however, is the most simple, natural mindfulness technique, because the breath is always happening in the here and now, and we always have it with us. It's coming from inside and outside of our bodies, and we can feel it in our bodies as it happens. So it provides a somewhat more physical, present support than just a visual or mental object. In mindfulness meditation, we don't try to manipulate the breath or breathe in a particular way. We simply use our natural breathing as a focal point, a resting place for our wandering mind.

· I HAVE SO MANY THOUGHTS; HOW CAN I GET RID OF THEM?

Thoughts are a natural part of the human mind and aren't rejected in mindfulness meditation. The goal is not to clear our minds or develop some kind of blank or "ideal" state, but rather to notice the alternation between getting caught in our habitual thoughts and coming back to rest in the present moment with our intended object of meditation. Sometimes your mind may seem very busy and full of thoughts, and at other times you may feel calm and more easily present. But in mindfulness meditation this doesn't matter all that much, because we are simply strengthening our ability to notice our habits and then come back to where we are. It's said that each time we notice our thoughts and return to our intended focus, we are accomplishing the practice. There is no other goal than this.

· HOW CAN I TELL IF I'M DOING IT RIGHT?

As long as you come back to your object of meditation when you notice that your mind has wandered, you're doing the practice. It doesn't matter how many times you do this during a session, because every time you do it you are accomplishing the practice. The only way you can do this practice wrong is if you notice you have wandered into thinking and decide to continue on with that rather than simply acknowledging it and returning to your breath.

DO I HAVE TO BELIEVE SOMETHING TO DO THIS MEDITATION?

Although mindfulness meditation comes from the Buddhist tradition, it doesn't involve any belief system other than trust in yourself. Even if you have strong "istic" beliefs (theistic, agnostic, atheistic, etc.) or are confused about the whole thing, you can sit on the earth with your own body and mind and develop more familiarity with yourself first-hand. You could say that mindfulness meditation is the opposite of having to believe in something, because you let thoughts and ideas go as you come back again and again to your own body and breath, and to your actual, present existence.

IS IT OKAY TO USE APPS TO MEDITATE?

Definitely. It's good to try different apps until you find one that works for you, in terms of length, the instructions given, the instructor's voice, the background music used, and so on. Whatever helps you to stop and do this valuable practice is good, because no matter what, it's just you sitting there with your own unique body, breath, and thoughts.

CAN I DO THIS ON MY OWN?

You can always do this on your own in formal and informal ways. If you have a relatively uncluttered place at home or at work where you can close the door and sit for a predetermined length of time (short or longer, up to you), that's great. You can do this on your own or using an app and some kind of timer. (There are more guidelines earlier in this book.) You can also practice mindfulness when you're walking, driving, gardening, cooking, or, really, anything else. Just notice when your mind has become absorbed in thoughts and return simply to what you're doing, with a sense of enjoyment, curiosity, and appreciation. You can also take a brief 'mindful pause' any time you remember that you're here, right now. Pause, observe yourself for a moment, breathe, and continue on. Every moment is an opportunity to be present. Having said all of that, it's also important to receive instruction from someone with experience, either privately or by attending a group.

˒ WHAT IF I CAN'T DO THIS EVERY DAY?

Most people find it difficult to meditate regularly, especially at first. We're so used to keeping busy, and it's hard to sit still and breathe, especially at home where we have lots of familiar distractions. Try short periods at times that work for you, even if you just focus on your breathing for a few minutes while you're sitting at your desk. Signing up for a formal group or individual session once a week is an important way to help get yourself to meditate, and writing times in on your calendar can also make it more likely that you will follow through. But don't worry–even the thought of meditating is a pause in your thinking process, a sudden remembrance of where you are right now. At that moment, just breathe a few times and notice how your body is feeling. Remember to look up at the sky, to feel your feet touching the ground when you're walking, and to appreciate the colors and flavors of the food you're eating. Meditate as much as you can, but don't worry.

˒ IS IT POINTLESS TO JUST DO IT ONCE A WEEK?

It's great to do it once a week. People who do this notice mindfulness increasing in their lives and an ability to gradually sit longer in silent meditation. If you can meditate more often, that's good, because it's the repetition that helps to internalize the habit of being more present and aware. But anything you can do makes a difference, and weekly sessions are effective.

ABOUT THE AUTHOR

Patricia Ullman holds a Juris Doctor (J.D.) degree and has spent her professional life in law, mediation, restorative justice, and non-profit leadership. She brings mindfulness techniques into these fields as part of the natural process of transforming organizational culture and working with conflict. Patricia is a senior teacher and meditation instructor in the Tibetan Buddhist tradition, having studied and practiced for over forty years under the guidance of some of the most renowned teachers of our day. She has been sharing her knowledge and experience for many years, leading workshops and retreats throughout Europe and North America for professionals, students, children, and adults.

Patricia spent many years as the Executive Director of an international retreat and program center in Nova Scotia and as the Director of Practice & Education for a similar retreat center in France. She also served as Executive Director of a community development non-profit in Halifax, Nova Scotia.

She lives in the Washington, DC area and works with private clients and groups who wish to gain tools for improving the quality of their lives and work. She is currently working toward a master's degree in counselling psychology.

Entering the Mainstream is Patricia's second book, following *Eight Steps to an Authentic Life: Ancient Wisdom for Modern Times.*

Made in the USA
Middletown, DE
01 December 2021

53926047R00109